Inclusive Education

Inclusive Education

A global agenda

Edited by Sip Jan Pijl,
Cor J. W. Meijer and
Seamus Hegarty

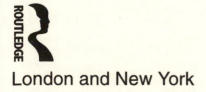

London and New York

First published 1997
by Routledge
11 New Fetter Lane, London EC4P 4EE

Simultaneously published in the USA and Canada
by Routledge
29 West 35th Street, New York, NY 10001

Typeset in Garamond by
Ponting–Green Publishing Services, Chesham,
Buckinghamshire
Printed and bound in Great Britain by
TJ Press (Padstow) Ltd, Padstow, Cornwall

British Library Cataloguing in Publication Data
A catalogue record for this book is available from the
British Library

Library of Congress Cataloging in Publication Data
Inclusive education: a global agenda / edited by Sip Jan Pijl,
    Cor J. W. Meijer, and Seamus Hegarty.
            p.   cm.
        Includes bibliographical references and index.
        1. Mainstreaming in education.   2. Handicapped children–
Education.   3. School management and organization.
    I. Pijl, S. J.   II. Meijer, Cor J. W.   III. Hegarty, Seamus.
    LC4015.I487   1997
    371.9'046–dc20   96–26329

ISBN   0–415–14748–4 (hbk)
ISBN   0–415–14749–2 (pbk)

Contents

Notes on contributors

Janice M. Baker (PhD) is an Assistant Professor of Special Education in Peabody College of Vanderbilt University, Tennessee. She is involved in research on educational services for students with behaviour disorders and learning disabilities, mainstreaming practices for students with learning disabilities, and comprehensive services for students with behavioural disorders. She is also a research scientist in the Kennedy Center at Vanderbilt University.

Alan Dyson (PhD) and **Alan Millward** (PhD) are co-Directors of the Special Needs Research Group in the Department of Education, University of Newcastle upon Tyne, England. They have recently undertaken a range of projects investigating current developments in special needs provision in the United Kingdom, including a survey of innovative provision for the Department for Education, a survey of specific learning difficulties provision for the Scottish Office, and a study of local education authorities' changing approaches to special needs. They both also have a substantial background as special needs teachers in mainstream and special schools.

Peter Evans (PhD) completed his PhD at the University of Manchester, Hester Adrian Research Centre in the field of special education. He subsequently became Senior Lecturer at the Institute of Education, University of London in the Department of Educational Psychology and Special Educational Needs. He then directed a research project, funded by the Department of Education and Science (United Kingdom), on curriculum development for pupils with moderate learning difficulties before moving to the Organization for Economic Co-operation and Development (OECD), in Paris, where he has responsibility for programmes on special education.

Bjørn Glæsel works as Chief School Psychologist in Copenhagen. Since 1955 he has worked as a teacher, college professor and school psychologist in the pedagogical, psychological and organizational aspects of special education. Since 1972 he has been editor of the *Danish Journal of School Psychology*.

Seamus Hegarty (PhD) is Director of the National Foundation for Educational Research in England and Wales. He has researched and written widely on special education, with a particular focus on integration. He is founder editor of the *European Journal of Special Needs Education* and editor of *Educational Research*. He has acted as consultant on special needs issues to UNESCO and numerous other national and international bodies.

Don Labon (PhD) is a self-employed educational consultant, a chartered psychologist and a Fellow of the British Psychological Society; his doctoral thesis was in the field of educational evaluation. Most of his international consultancy work is for the Organization for Economic Co-operation and Development (OECD) and this has included editing the first part and writing the second of the publication providing the main information bases for his chapter. Previously he was employed in England by the Department for Education as Her Majesty's Inspectorate's Staff Inspector with national responsibilities for special needs at all stages of education, and for teacher training and higher education. Earlier posts included university lecturer and Principal Educational Psychologist for a local education authority.

Cor J. W. Meijer (PhD) is the co-ordinator of a nationwide evaluation of the current integration policy in the Netherlands and is as such attached to the Institute for Educational Research, SVO, in The Hague. He has conducted several studies on special and regular education. He is mainly involved in comparative research on special needs education and integration. He is a member of the OECD/CERI group of experts for the project 'Integration in the school'.

Sip Jan Pijl (PhD) is senior researcher at GION, the Groningen Institute for Educational Research, University of Groningen, the Netherlands. He is involved in studies on the integration of students with special needs into regular education and has conducted international comparative research on integration. He is a member of the Groningen Centre for Comparative Education and a member of an international network for inclusive education.

Gordon L. Porter (PhD) is Director of Student Services for School District 12 in Woodstock, New Brunswick, Canada. He is internationally known for both advocacy and leadership in creating inclusionary school programmes. He has written several articles and chapters on inclusive education and has delivered papers and seminars on this topic. Gordon Porter has served as national president of the Canadian Association for Community Living and continues to work actively on educational issues through CACL and Inclusion International. He has taught at the McGill University Summer Institute in Integrated Education since 1990 as well as at the University of Calgary and was a Visiting Fellow at the New Zealand Institute of Mental Retardation at the University of Otago.

Mårten Söder (PhD) is Professor of Sociology at the University of Bergen, Norway and the University of Uppsala, Sweden. He has over the years completed several projects about the changes in Scandinavian welfare states and their implications for disadvantaged groups.

Gunnar Stangvik (PhD) is Professor of Education at Finmark College, Alta, Norway, and Adjunct Professor of Education at the University of Trondheim. His research has covered a number of special education issues: reading, efficacy of special education, self-concept development and evaluation. He has written several books on inclusion.

Luc M. Stevens (PhD) is Professor of Special Education at the University of Utrecht, the Netherlands. His main subjects of interest are classroom motivation, teacher–pupil interaction and school ethos, and early identification of and intervention with educationally at-risk children. Currently, he is strongly involved in a nationwide integration project and is a member of the committee in charge of evaluating this project.

Naomi Zigmond (PhD) is Chair of the Department of Instruction and Learning and Professor of Special Education in the School of Education at the University of Pittsburgh, USA. She has conducted numerous research studies on integration of students with disabilities into general education classrooms, transition from school to work, students with disabilities who drop out of school, and preparation of general and special education teachers.

Preface and acknowledgements

Special education is conceived differently in different parts of the world and practice varies accordingly. The familiar variation in the use made of special schools is just one example of the diversity that characterizes special educational provision globally. However, there are some convergences and one of the most significant of these relates to inclusive education.

The language of special education is not static and recent years have seen major debates successively take place around mainstreaming, integration and inclusion. These concepts are in fact not as sharply delimited from each other as some protagonists maintain, but what has been emerging, regardless of the language used, is a clearer focus on an educational reform agenda. The provision of high quality education for all pupils is increasingly located within a school reform context and to that extent pupils with special needs are naturally encompassed within a common framework of significant educational action.

Given that inclusive education is the goal, how do we achieve it? This was the leading question at a conference in Rotterdam, the Netherlands. The conference was organized by the Dutch process management Weer Samen Naar School ('together to school again'). The process management's task is to support the development towards inclusive education in the Netherlands. A number of distinguished researchers contributed to the conference and afterwards they, together with a few others, were invited to contribute to a book about inclusion.

This book assembles arguments and practical examples from around the globe in order to clarify the rationale for inclusion and to demonstrate how it is put into practice. Drawing on national and international data, it offers a cogent and informative text that will inform those many people concerned with this central issue.

ACKNOWLEDGEMENTS

We should like to express our gratitude to the Dutch organization Procesmanagement Weer Samen Naar School for their grant for the writing of this book. We also wish to thank Conny Lenderink for her editorial support.

Sip Jan Pijl
Cor J. W. Meijer
Seamus Hegarty

Chapter 1

Introduction

*Cor J. W. Meijer, Sip Jan Pijl and
Seamus Hegarty*

INCLUSION

For decades special schools have been the pivot of the education of
pupils with special needs. In quite a number of countries in the
Western world, educators and administrators have put a great deal
of effort into the development of a thorough and widely accepted
system of special schools. In these schools all the available expertise
has been concentrated in an attempt to educate pupils with special
needs in the best way. Because of the unusual, special instruction
provided in these schools many function as separate, independent
schools. Since the 1920s the separate system for special education has
been enlarged and refined.

The separate system used to be seen as an expression of the care
for pupils with special needs. However, this view of special education
has gradually changed. Knowledge, expertise and facilities are still of
importance to the education of pupils with special needs, but the
segregation of these pupils is now perceived as unacceptable. The
prevailing view is that they should be educated together with their
peers in regular education settings. The consequence is that regular
and special education as separate systems disappear and are replaced
by a single system that includes a wide range of pupils. In such an
'inclusive' system all pupils attend in principle the same school. The
term 'inclusive education' stands for an educational system that
includes a large diversity of pupils and which differentiates education
for this diversity.

The term 'inclusion' has a wider context than the term 'integration'. Integration reflects the attempts to place pupils with special
needs in the mainstream in regular education. Several authors (Jordan
and Powell 1994; Söder 1989, 1991) have pointed out that integration
is often seen as re-integration after a period of segregation, or as a

means to avoid segregation. Integration then may result in attempts to adapt an existing mainstream curriculum in order to meet the pupils' special needs. Integration in its most negative connotation stands for integration by location, whilst providing a watered-down variant of the regular curriculum.

Of course integration should not be about where pupils are placed nor about providing access to pre-set norms of learning and behaviour; it is about fitting schools to meet the needs of all their pupils (Hegarty 1991). This wider notion of integration comes close to the concept of inclusion. In this book the terms integration and inclusion are both used according to countries' habits and authors' preferences. Both terms are used to express comparable processes and outcomes. A number of authors explicitly address the different terminologies and clarify their points of view (see, for instance, Stangvik, and Dyson and Millward in chapters 4 and 5).

In many countries the effort to achieve a more inclusive system has resulted in the education of special needs pupils in regular schools and in a declining number of pupils placed in separate, special schools (Pijl and Meijer 1991). In other countries, such as the Netherlands, Belgium and Germany, this development has been considerably slower or even absent. In the last three countries, for instance, over 3 per cent of all pupils, aged 6 to 17, are placed full-time in a separate, special school. In other countries, like Sweden, England and the United States, these percentages are considerably lower – well under 2 per cent. A study conducted by the OECD (1995a) shows that half of the countries in the OECD educate less than 1 per cent of their pupils in special schools.

The attempts to realize more inclusive education have resulted in very different educational arrangements in different countries. In the last few years quite a number of comparative studies have been conducted in which various aspects of inclusive education have been described (Broekaert and Bradt 1995; Commissie van de Europese Gemeenschappen 1992; Daniels and Hogg 1992; Leijser et al. 1994; Lynch 1994; Meijer et al. 1994; Norwich 1994; OECD 1995a; O'Hanlon 1993; UNESCO 1994b; Walton et al. 1989). Given the number of studies that focus on inclusion, one can conclude that researchers and the bodies funding them expect to gain new insights from international comparisons that will assist in the process of finding solutions for common problems. These comparative studies normally consist of a number of country descriptions in which legislation, regulations, organization and the practice of inclusion are described. After the country descriptions, an attempt is made to draw some general conclusions based on them. These studies focus attention on the extent to which problems are common across countries and on the existence of general solutions.

The question is not only whether the assumption is true that problems are common across countries, but also what the general findings exactly are and to what degree they contain solutions for other countries. The above studies are largely descriptive and take into account the (national) context in which the educational processes take place. Although these studies are generally interesting, informative and sometimes surprising, it should be noted that the conclusions often simply repeat the country differences already discussed. The integration of the cross-country findings into a set of new hypotheses or a theory on integration obviously causes great difficulty.

It is important to note that in these studies there is considerable scope for subjective interpretation. The researcher determines the facts to be described, the conclusions to be drawn and to that extent the quality of the comparisons drawn. That is at least partly due to the fact that countries and their education systems differ from each other in so many aspects that it is always possible to find differences that seem to be linked to the dependent variables under consideration. This in turn makes it difficult to draw general conclusions from comparative research, and it explains why comparative research reports are often read just to learn something about another country or to search for novel systems and practices that are worth introducing in one's own system. The study of other countries' systems highlights the differences between them and frequently throws up ideas for improving provision in one's own country. However, these generally only work if certain conditions have been met: for instance, a certain teacher–pupil ratio, extra support available in the school and one law for special and regular education. Next to these conditions in education there are other conditions, like for instance a particular country's history in integration, the low population density resulting in large distances between schools and the single school system. Practices in other countries may work in that particular context, but it is unlikely that these practices will work as well in a different context. Making use of experiences other countries have in integration is very often not simply a matter of copying practices.

Other comparative approaches are found in the 'Education at a Glance' studies of the OECD (OECD 1995b), the IEA studies (International Association for the Evaluation of Educational

Achievement; Elley 1992, 1994) or the NCEO studies (National Center on Educational Outcomes 1993a, 1993b). These studies focus on the outcomes of educational processes and try to relate outcomes to resources (input and context). It is argued that the emphasis on educational reform and accountability reflects the general wish to measure pupil achievement and how it is related to various indicators (NCEO 1993a, 1993b). In these studies not only are general descriptions given of the educational systems in different countries or states, but also cross-country comparisons are made in terms of input, context and output variables. Although these studies meet the criterion of objectivity, there is some criticism of the comparability of the findings. Wielemans (1995) refers to these studies as context-exclusive comparisons, based on statistical information. According to him, the comparability of this type of study is often weak and the conclusions often misleading.

Wielemans (1995) prefers context-inclusive studies, in which the historical, socio-economic, political, geographical, cultural and religious contexts are taken into account. He argues that these context-inclusive studies should require 'equivalence'. Meijer *et al.* (1994) define this concept as follows: 'equivalence focuses on the relationships between a general dimension – for instance: a concept like social integration – and different indicators for it – for instance: placement in regular education and teacher attitudes' (Meijer *et al.* 1994: 3).

> Equivalence implies that the same set of indicators relates to the general dimension. Equivalence is absent if a concept in different countries relates to different sets of indicators. In fact, we then have two different theories to explain our concept, and comparative research really becomes difficult then. In this view, comparability requires a theoretical underpinning in which the relationships between the variables of interest to the researcher are related to each other. A comparative analysis only makes sense if this theory can be applied in each of the countries involved.
>
> (Meijer *et al.* 1994: 3)

Wielemans (1995) stresses that equivalence can only be achieved by developing a broad and multidisciplinary knowledge base of the contextual factors. Only then is comparability possible.

Our position comes close to what Wielemans refers to as the study of relations between relations (Wielemans 1995: 28). It is not the country that is the unit of comparison in this book, nor units within countries. The really useful experiences are not those which are easy to describe. What can be found in other countries is information about the factors relevant in realizing inclusion in education. So, comparative research does not end with the description of practices in other countries. Its interest is also in knowledge about the relevant factors in integration. It is, for instance, interesting to know that in Sweden working units have a special teacher, that in Denmark many pupils with learning disabilities go to a 'clinic' and that schools in the United States have a resource room, but what really contributes to our understanding of inclusion is that the successful inclusion of pupils with special needs depends on having a (part-time) instruction facility outside the classroom.

Comparative research should contribute to our knowledge of the effects of different arrangements in inclusive education. The question here is which factors in inclusion are relevant in realizing inclusive education. Niessen and Peschar (1982) describe this question as the third purpose of comparative research: a purpose that follows theoretical interests. A more general question then is: what theoretically relevant relationships can be specified (Niessen and Peschar 1982; Øyen 1990).

The chapters which follow focus on the relation between inclusion and the factors that are assumed to be related to or predict the success of inclusion. We do not set out to describe systems in different countries and we are also not concerned with the contextual differences in which inclusion takes place. Our interest is purely theoretical: the development of a theory that focuses on the factors (at various levels) that have a major influence on the success of inclusion.

In this book an unusual angle of incidence has been applied to investigate the factors that are relevant to the case for inclusion in schools. The book does not consist simply of a number of country descriptions with an integrating chapter, but of invited contributions describing the factors relevant for inclusion from leading authors in the field. The authors were asked to prepare a chapter which systematically addressed a number of potentially relevant factors. We asked them to react to a paper by the editors on factors that might be relevant in making education inclusive. The express intention was that they deal with that issue without detailing contextual differences or differences in educational approaches. Although the authors are from different countries and make some references to the practices in their own countries, each chapter can be read as an analysis of factors relevant for realizing inclusive education. These analyses are written with a wide range of expertise.

CONTENT OF THE BOOK

The book addresses the question: what factors are relevant to implementing inclusion in education? In the second chapter a number of potentially relevant factors are presented. It is assumed that inclusive education depends on what teachers do in classrooms, on the way in which schools organize their curriculum and on a number of factors outside schools. These three levels make up the framework for the book and elements from this framework can be found in most of the essays contained in it.

In the following chapters a wider perspective on the questions posed is taken. In chapter 3 Söder distinguishes two categories of questions in research on inclusion. Evaluative questions examine the effects of inclusion, whereas normative questions address the good examples of inclusion practices. Söder argues that inclusion should be accepted as an overall goal and research can contribute to that goal by taking neither the evaluative nor the normative perspective, but by asking questions aimed at understanding and improving the position of handicapped people. In chapter 4, Stangvik puts inclusion in education in the wider perspective of policy and changes in society. Inclusion is more than a school problem: it has to do with people's lives outside school, with family and with community. Inclusion is not just the implementation of a new learning arrangement; it demands innovation and reform of schools.

Dyson and Millward in chapter 5 narrow the discussion down to two paradigms in education, the 'psycho-medical' paradigm and the 'interactive' paradigm. Working from these two conflicting paradigms either leads to the adoption of (separate) special education provision or to the implementation of inclusive education. Dyson and Millward argue, as Stangvik and others do, that national governments only set the context for a policy, while local policy-makers, schools and teachers determine what actually goes on in classrooms. If schools decide on inclusive education they in fact have to implement changes at all levels in the school.

In chapters 6 to 11, several factors relevant to the realization of inclusive education have been worked out. Based on experiences in Canada, Porter goes into a number of leadership factors, the new role for the special educator and possible strategies for supporting the teacher in the regular classroom. Labon presents an overview of recent work undertaken by the OECD. Based on individual reports on special needs provision in twenty-four countries, he selects the key issues at the classroom, school and national levels. In the United States the Regular Education Initiative gave new momentum to the inclusion of pupils with disabilities in educational programmes with non-disabled peers. Zigmond and Baker present studies of four experimental models of full inclusion and draw the lessons to be learned from these experiments. In so doing, they define inclusion as a fundamental reform of the mainstream, discuss the special needs provisions available in the United States and address the expanding role of the special education teacher.

Meijer and Stevens analyse the factors that contribute to the maintenance of segregated forms of special education for those with learning disabilities and mild mental retardation in the Netherlands. They argue that these factors can be seen as inhibiting factors in inclusion. They point out that the mere existence of separate legislation, funding regulations and school systems, the isolated position of many (small) schools and the uniform curriculum have been factors in provoking referrals. Evans too focuses on the largest group of special needs pupils, the children with learning difficulties. He starts with an analysis of the way in which children with learning difficulties learn in schools and, based on this analysis, formulates practical implications in terms of skills, resources, time and policy development. Glæsel discusses inclusion of severely handicapped pupils in Denmark. Practically all other pupils attend regular education. The inclusion of severely handicapped pupils demands a lot in terms of teacher training and the arrangements in education. Glæsel elaborates a number of these conditions.

In the final chapter by Meijer, Pijl and Hegarty the key elements from the different contributions made in this book have been extracted. In this chapter the question as to what factors are relevant in the implementation of inclusive education is taken up again. The authors point out that realizing inclusion largely depends on a basis in society and on parental pressure, on a conducive policy, on decentralization and on conceptualizing inclusion as a school reform.

Chapter 2

Factors in inclusion: a framework

Sip Jan Pijl and Cor J. W. Meijer

INTRODUCTION

In the past decades an impressive number of publications on inclusion have been written, not always with 'inclusion' as the central concept, but also using concepts like 'mainstreaming' or 'integration'. These publications address a wide variety of subjects: the philosophy behind inclusion, the necessary requirements for inclusion, the effects on inclusion for pupils, parents, schools and teachers, etc. In most of these publications one or more factors considered relevant for realizing an inclusive school are put forward, for instance: a much more differentiated curriculum, teacher support teams, legislation and regulations supporting inclusion. Studies show that minor adaptations in the regular curriculum can easily lead to would-be inclusion, that a teacher support team and intensive staff development make teachers more self-confident and willing to accept a special needs pupil, and that new legislation affects the referral behaviour of schools.

It is obvious that an almost endless list of essential steps to take, of necessary conditions to fulfil and of desired ways of working can be compiled from these publications. Each of these dos and don'ts can be rewritten in terms of the factors relevant for making education inclusive. For most of these factors it seems plausible that they contribute to realizing an inclusive school, but as yet we lack convincing evidence about their relevance. Studies show that certain innovations or changes do have an effect, but the link with inclusive education is often indirect and partial. At the same time it is clear that none of these are in themselves enough to realize inclusion. Inclusive education depends on the implementation of a set of related factors, with the proviso that several sets consisting of slightly differing factors may do the job. This certainly holds for different countries, but also within one country there are probably many roads leading to Rome.

A search for one or two key factors that make up inclusion can therefore be regarded as unrealistic. In this book we aim for the selection of those factors that form an integral part of most sets. Alternatively, we seek to answer the question: what are the minimum conditions for realizing inclusive education?

The contributors to this book were invited to write a chapter about the factors they considered to be relevant. In order to explain what was meant by the term 'factor' and to provide some structure for the authors, a framework was developed in which three groups of factors were described: it is assumed that inclusive education depends on what teachers do in classrooms, on the way in which schools organize their education and on a number of factors outside schools.

Teacher factors

The way in which teachers realize inclusion in the classroom largely depends on their attitude towards pupils with special needs and on the resources available to them. In quite a number of studies the attitude of teachers towards educating pupils with special needs has been put forward as a decisive factor in making schools more inclusive (Hegarty 1994). If regular teachers do not accept the education of these pupils as an integral part of their job, they will try to make someone else (often the special teacher) responsible for these pupils and will organize covert segregation in the school (e.g., the special class).

The different types of resources available to teachers can be deduced from the micro-economics of teaching (Brown and Saks 1980; Gerber and Semmel 1985). In these theories the term 'resources' does not only refer to teaching methods and materials, but also to time available for instruction and to the knowledge and skills of teachers acquired through training and experience. All these resources can be used for education.

Teaching pupils with special needs in the regular classroom no doubt deviates from the 'regular' programme. Teachers are confronted with the question of how to instruct these pupils. Special needs pupils may require more instruction time or other learning methods and professional knowledge. In which case, teachers will feel the need to expand their resources: more time, materials and knowledge. The problem is that teachers may have limited access to additional resources. These are relatively scarce and fixed (Gerber and Semmel 1985). Of course this does not hold true for all resources. Learning materials are relatively easy to borrow and photocopy, but it is more expensive to purchase new methods or create room to work in smaller groups. Increasing available time or enhancing teachers' professional knowledge is also often very expensive. Less expensive ways of creating more time (e.g., education assistants) and enhancing professional knowledge in schools (e.g., consultation teams) are of limited availability. The outcome of these considerations is that, given finite resources, teachers need to rearrange available resources across the pupils in the classroom. Teachers, for instance, can encourage above-average pupils to work more independently, to work with computers and to help each other, so that more teaching time is left for special needs pupils.

To realize the inclusion of these pupils in regular education, teachers will try to enhance the amount of resources and differentiate between pupils with respect to the amount and type of resources available to them. The idea is that a successful inclusion of special needs pupils not only depends on appropriate organization, legislation and regulations, but also on the availability of resources in the regular classroom and on the way teachers differentiate the resources between pupils.

In summary, teachers' attitudes, available instruction time, the knowledge and skills of teachers and the teaching methods and materials on hand seem to be important prerequisites for special needs teaching in regular settings.

School factors

Next to the attitudes of teachers and the availability and quality of resources in the classroom there are factors at the school level and at the district or national level that may influence the factors at the teacher level. These factors can operate as prerequisites for changing attitudes and for putting resources into education.

The basic question concerning the organization necessary for educating special needs pupils in regular schools is how the special services are to be provided. In a review of studies on integration, Hegarty et al. (1981) give an overview of the organizational structure of integration:

(a)   regular class, no support;
(b)   regular class, in-class support for teacher and/or pupils;
(c)   regular class, pull-out support;
(d)   regular class as basis, part-time special class;
(e)   special class as basis, part-time regular class;
(f)   full-time special class;
(g)   part-time special school, part-time regular school;
(h)   full-time special school.

The above-mentioned variants give the possible forms in which integration can be organized. A characteristic of variant (b) is that support can be provided for the regular teacher and special needs pupil in the regular classroom. In all other forms special needs pupils are given assistance in a special setting. Extra support can be very different: for example, a special teacher for pupils with reading difficulties, a computer for pupils having problems with arithmetic, extra support for the class teacher with pupils with behaviour problems.

Each point on this continuum can be elaborated in various ways and each has its own advantages and disadvantages for different groups of special needs pupils. It is obvious that the level of integration varies with each variant. With variants (a), (b) and (c), social, curricular or psychological integration (as defined by Kobi 1983) seems achievable, while with variants (e), (f) and (g), lower levels of integration (physical, administrative) will be realized (Kobi 1983). Because the organizational structure can determine the resources teachers can use in teaching children with special needs, it is clearly an important issue in further policy decisions on inclusion. It largely sets the conditions for teaching special needs pupils.

The special school system has already been mentioned while describing the organizational structure. The role of special schools and special teachers can be elaborated on further. The experience, knowledge and facilities of the special school system can be made available to regular schools in various ways. Other means of support, such as special needs teams, libraries with information on teaching methods and materials as well as therapists, should also provide assistance to regular schools.

In studies describing the organization of educational systems in other countries (see, for instance, Meijer *et al.* 1994), concepts such as 'decentralization', 'flexibility' and 'authorization to decide' seem to be linked to successfully integrating special needs pupils into regular schools. These concepts stand for increasing the power to take decisions concerning special help within schools.

A final aspect of organization is co-operation between (regular) schools. Currently the formation of clusters of schools is seen in the Netherlands under the so-called 'Weer samen naar school' policy and similar developments occur in the United Kingdom (Dyson and Gains 1993; Lunt *et al.* 1994; Meijer 1995). It is clear that the creative strengths, knowledge and expertise, as well as the facilities, of a group of schools exceed those of a single school. The ability of co-operating schools to find ways of taking care of special needs may be essential for integrating special needs pupils into regular settings. On the other hand, it is easy to imagine that organizing such co-operation requires valuable time and may lead to bureaucracy.

In summary, the issues involved in organizing inclusive education at the school level are: (1) a structure for providing special services in schools; (2) the role of special education; (3) other support systems; (4) decentralization; and (5) co-operation between schools.

External factors

A number of factors outside schools and outside education affect daily school practice. Legislation, regulations, and funding provide the framework within which schools can operate. As a rule, laws and (financial) regulations do not run counter to public opinion and often government legislation follows developments in society (Elmore 1989). Thus, prevailing public opinion on the position of special education and the pupils attending it determine – via laws and (financial) regulations – the way in which special needs teaching in regular education has been realized.

Even if society is in favour of integration, it does not necessarily imply that teachers hold similar views. After all they have to realize integration in everyday school practice under certain conditions. They may well have to consider whether having special needs pupils in regular classrooms is in the interest of these pupils themselves and perhaps whether it is disadvantageous to other pupils in the class (Schumm and Vaughn 1991; Whinnery *et al.* 1991).

In summary, it seems worthwhile to take into account public opinion and the attendant legislation, regulations and funding as determining factors for providing special needs provision in regular education. A special point of interest here is whether the views of teachers run parallel to those in society.

THE MAIN QUESTIONS

The factors mentioned above are potentially relevant to special needs teaching in regular schools. At the classroom level we distinguished the available instruction time, the knowledge and skills of teachers, the teaching methods and the materials on hand as important prerequisites for special needs teaching in regular settings. The issues involved in organizing inclusive education at the school level are: (1) a structure for providing special services in schools; (2) the role of special education; (3) other support systems; (4) decentralization; and (5) co-operation between schools. With respect to factors outside schools it is worthwhile to take into account public opinion and the attendant legislation, regulations and funding as determining factors for providing special needs provision in regular education.

The contributors to this book have been invited to address these issues. A central question is whether the issues mentioned above are relevant to the inclusion of special needs pupils in regular education. And if they are, what should be done? Specifically, what would be the advice to policy-makers, teacher educators, school support services, schools, etc., in countries trying to realize or to improve inclusive education? What seem to be sensible first steps, taking into account limited means?

It is obvious that not all contributors address all the possible factors mentioned above. Depending on personal interests, knowledge and current developments in different countries, each contributor has chosen to go into a limited number of issues regarded as most relevant in making schools inclusive and – in a number of cases – to insert new factors. There is no presumption of being exhaustive, but the essays which follow contain an overview of current thinking on the factors that promote or inhibit inclusive education.

Chapter 3

A research perspective on integration

Mårten Söder

INTRODUCTION

For more than a decade, researchers have been engaged in questions related to integrating the disabled. The main research questions have been evaluative (is integration good or bad?) and normative (how to make integration work). Although some knowledge about integration has been generated from these perspectives, research has failed to come up with any definite answer to the questions posed. In this chapter I will argue that neither the evaluative nor the normative questions are very fruitful ones. They tend to trap researchers into asking questions about segregation–integration that blind them to more relevant ones. Research gets caught up in a debate on integration that cannot – by its very nature – be answered by research. By accepting the idea that 'we' are integrating 'them', the research focus is narrowed down to questions of whether 'we' are doing the right thing or how 'we' should do it. This prevents us from asking other basic questions about the lives of the disabled.

The idea of integration grew out of criticism of traditional institutions. Integration, in a broad and somewhat diffuse sense, can therefore be looked upon as the antithesis of institutions (including special schools) and all they stand for: inclusion rather than exclusion, choice and participation rather than restrictions and isolation. Integration thus stands for all those things that the mentally retarded have been denied in segregated institutions.

I will use the concepts 'integration' and 'community integration' in a broad sense, although when understood as the antithesis of traditional institutions, it is perhaps not surprising that people usually associate community integration with living and housing arrangements. But integration or mainstreaming in schools is also part of the ambition to integrate the disabled into the community, as are different forms of integration at work, family support and other daily activities. 'Integration' as used here thus includes integration in all these different spheres.

Most of the research I will be referring to is about people with developmental disabilities, though I see no reason to doubt that my argument is also valid for research on integrating people with other disabilities.

DIFFERENT PERSPECTIVES

That research has not come up with any definite answer to the question of integration is shown by the fact that one can find support for almost any opinion on the issue in research literature. Different researchers use different perspectives to interpret the reality they are studying. Even if they agree on the basic meaning of things, their approaches and perspectives make them interpret what they see in different ways.

For example, in an overview of deinstitutionalization research it is stated that:

> A consensus is emerging that as a wide-spread social movement, deinstitutionalization has been less than successful in addressing the major issues reflected in its ideology base and that this failure occurs across many targeted populations. All too often community services conspire to re-enact the very same institutional processes of ensuring the physical and social isolation and stigmatization of handicapped persons, maintaining the asymmetrical power relationships between residents and staff and encouraging dependency and regimentation.
>
> (Emerson 1985: 282)

This rather negative picture can be contrasted with what is said in a report on a meeting in Washington, where several researchers and practitioners set out to summarize and evaluate what we know about community integration:

> All people with developmental disabilities, including those with severe developmental behavioral and health impairments can live successfully in the community if appropriately supported ... The evidence and experience indicate that life in the community is better than life in institutions in terms of relationships, family

contact, frequency and diversity of relationships, individual development and leisure, recreational and spiritual resources.

(From Being in the Community . . . 1988: 4)

Reviewing the same field of research and to a certain extent even the same research, different reviewers draw different conclusions. The same contradiction can be found in overviews of research on integration in schools. While some reviewers emphasize that no substantial effects in terms of model learning, better self-image or attitudes among peers have occurred (Gottlieb 1981; Zigler and Hoddap 1986), others conclude that results are generally promising to that end (Hegarty 1982).

This conflict in interpreting research and evaluating research findings can be explained partly by a distinction between two different perspectives. These have been referred to as a discipline-oriented perspective versus a policy-oriented one (Bruininks 1990), and a social science perspective versus a civil rights one (Gow *et al.* 1988), or as a research perspective versus an advocacy perspective (Menolascino and Stark 1990). In order to avoid these somewhat value-laden terms, I will refer to the first one as an evaluative perspective and the second as a normative perspective.

The difference between the perspectives goes back to how one sees and evaluates segregated institutions. Basically, the criticism of such institutions was, and is, based on two different types of argument. The first one relates to the negative effects of segregative measures. Much research has documented these effects on the personal development of the client: his or her learning ability, emotional development, adaptive behaviour and self-image. Consequently, alternatives are promoted which are expected to have more positive, or at least fewer negative, effects in this regard and are judged according to their effects on the disabled person.

The second or normative perspective criticizes institutions on other grounds. Segregation is seen as violating basic values and rights. Segregation means denying people their right to lead normal lives. It violates basic values of equality, freedom and choice and stands in direct contrast to ideas of 'a society for all' and 'a school for all'. Seen in this perspective, integration as an alternative is good because it accords with these basic values. The alternatives should therefore not be judged primarily in terms of their effects on the disabled, but according to how well they live up to the values of 'equality' and 'freedom'.

The logic in this kind of reasoning might sound unscientific, especially in relation to the first argument about individual effects, but it is a logic that we often apply to politics and ideology. To take a simple example from another field: when we are discussing equality between the sexes, equality is usually seen as a value in, and of, itself. We do not promote it by arguing that equal wages or equal opportunity have good effects on the personal development or adaptive behaviour of women. This is essentially the same way the normative perspective argues in relation to integrating disabled people.

The different ways of looking at segregation and what is wrong with it have implications for the kind of research questions asked about integration. I will use this distinction between the evaluative and the normative perspective to give some examples of research done within each perspective, before discussing their common shortcomings and alternative approaches.

Evaluation

If you are interested in the effects of integration on a mentally retarded person, the question you ask is whether these are positive or negative. Thus integration has to prove itself, so to speak.

Deinstitutionalization and integration are seen as natural experiments. The role of research is to answer the question of whether life in a community has positive or negative effects on an individual. Living and school arrangements are seen as independent variables whose effects on the disabled person should be scientifically assessed. In order to ascertain these effects, researchers try to measure them as objectively as possible. The ideal research setting for this is in an experiment where external factors can be kept under control and a control group can help assess the influence of the independent variable. But pure experiments cannot, for practical as well as ethical reasons, be performed. Research designs are created that as closely as possible resemble those of the pure experiment.

A lot of research has been done within this perspective. To begin with, the most common criterion – the variable used to measure effects – seems to have been the adaptive behaviour of the disabled person. The results are inconclusive, partly because the measures used have been rather crude, partly because adaptive behaviour is in itself a many-sided characteristic for which no generally accepted single definition exists. Later studies have focused on other criteria, for example activity. Often activity has been measured as the degree to which the disabled person uses ordinary facilities in the community. Although perhaps not a revolutionary finding – by definition segregation means that access to these facilities is restricted – studies in several countries show that community living often promotes using such community resources (Allen 1990; Halliday and Woolnough 1989; Schalock *et al.* 1981).

During the 1980s researchers have moved away from single person-centred characteristics as the criteria for measuring outcomes of community integration. Three developments can be noticed. The first is the insight that single measures, like adaptive behaviour, are insufficient. Adjustment to community is far too complex a process to be captured by one single dimension (Söder 1987). It has been suggested, based on the analysis of extensive data, that at least four dimensions of personal competence (personal independence, mal-adaptive behaviour, physical mobility and physical complications) and four dimensions of community adjustment (social-recreation-leisure, need for social support, economic integration and financial independence) are needed to describe the process of community integration (Bruininks 1990).

The second trend consists of a growing focus on the quality of life as an outcome measure. Behavioural and competence measures are not enough. Rather an account of the quality of the total life situation of a mentally retarded person is needed. In this account the way in which a person experiences this is an important aspect. The research focus has thus moved from behavioural outcomes to the effect of integration on the total, subjective as well as objective, life situation (Cattermole *et al.* 1990).

The third development concerns the difficulties in comparing institutional life with life in the community. There are huge vari-ations in the circumstances under which different institutions oper-ate and in what constitutes community living. Several researchers have therefore tried to substitute the single dichotomy, institution versus community, with more elaborate measures of the environ-ment. An ambition to capture variations in organizational, physical and more subtle characteristics like programming strategies, atti-tudes and social networks is characteristic of this trend, which is sometimes referred to as the 'person–environment' fit model.

To a large extent though, research which has focused on the effects of community integration has failed to come up with any definite answer to the evaluative question it poses: is community integration good or bad? This is not to deny that we have learned something about the specific conditions under which the behaviour of people with varying degrees of disability will be affected in different ways.

At the same time it is important to notice that most of the research projects that depart from the evaluative perspective fail to live up to the requirements of their own tradition. In overview articles complaints are legion: people studied have not been randomly selected; control groups are lacking, or have not been appropriately matched; definitions of central criterion variables are inconsistent between researchers; and the definition of independent variables is often lacking in distinctiveness (Gow *et al.* 1988).

Another way of saying this is that social reality has refused to let itself be formatted in the way scientific researchers want it to be. The question is whether it ever will. The methodological problems are so huge that one can have strong doubts as to whether this tradition will ever be able to answer the evaluative question it sets itself, that is whether community integration is good or bad.

The general answer to this question is, therefore, 'it depends'. The success of integrated living depends on the characteristics of the person being integrated, the type of housing area, attitudes of neighbours, flexibility of staff, social structure of the environment and so on (Mansell and Beasly 1990). The success of integration in school depends on the school climate, characteristics of teachers, teaching style, attitudes of peers and so on (Johnsson and Johnson 1984; Marchesi *et al.* 1991), in which case, maybe we should start looking at the factors themselves on which it depends. Maybe we have to abandon the idea that these are only important as independent variables. In other words, maybe the whole idea of objective measures of outcomes of integration is an obstacle to seeing and studying the things that are important in the lives of disabled people.

Normative research

Let us turn to the other perspective, which I call the normative one. In this perspective, community integration in itself does not have to be evaluated. It is right because it is in accordance with the basic values outlined above. The basic question asked in research is therefore not about the effects on the mentally retarded person, but about how we should make community integration true to these basic values. The issue of whether or not to integrate is not on the research agenda. But the question of how to accomplish integration certainly is. Research within this perspective is often focused on finding good examples, the ones where integration works according to expectations, and in trying to describe the practices that account for this success.

A comparative project run by the OECD (OECD 1985, 1986, 1988, 1991) is a case in point. Several innovative practices from different countries were identified, described and analysed by researchers and practitioners. School integration in Italy (Ferro 1985), case management in Denmark and Sweden (Boyd Kjellen *1991; Hultkvist 1991), supported employment in the United States and integration at work in Genoa, Italy (OECD 1986), are all examples of such innovative practices that have been identified and analysed in this project.

At the same time the project illustrates some problems with this approach. Good examples are not easily reproduced. One might learn something about how things can be done, but often there are so many cultural determinants that are difficult to grasp and manipulate that simple replication is almost impossible.

Similar studies analysing good practices can also be found in literature on mainstreaming and integration in schools (Hegarty 1982; Johnsson and Johnson 1984).

One of the merits of the normative approach is therefore that we can learn something from successful integration practices. The drawback is that we seldom get to learn about the problems. Because integration is assumed to be good from the beginning, there is a tendency not to talk about any disadvantages. Reality is seen as an arena for action but we need to know how to act on that reality to bring it into accordance with our goals, rather than look for information that might cast doubts on these goals.

THE IMPORTANCE OF ASKING THE RIGHT QUESTIONS

The different results emphasized in the aforementioned summaries can thus be explained by the fact that those responsible for the summaries apply different perspectives, both of which have their merits and shortcomings. The shortcoming of both is that they are each, in their own way, tied into the question of and controversy over whether integration is good or bad. They mirror the debate about institutions and special schools that has been going on in most developed countries over the last twenty years. This means they mirror a reality that is twenty years old and fail to address the reality of the present.

The question of whether community integration is good or bad cannot be answered definitely within either of these perspectives. In order to understand the process of integration, therefore, we have to ask new questions, questions that can help us understand the realities of the 1990s. We have to accept that science will never provide a simple and straightforward definite answer as to whether community integration works or not. Some people would even say it is not a scientific question in the first place. Certainly, politicians and decision-makers are not waiting for researchers to provide an answer before deciding their policies. Social politics is simply not determined in this way.

Today's reality is different from twenty years ago. More and more disabled people are living in the community. By implementing integration within the school system we have a generation of youngsters with disabilities that have never been segregated and for whom the idea of segregation – including that of integration – has no meaning to which they can relate. Society itself has changed. We are facing new situations and problems, and so of course are those people with disabilities living in that changed and changing society. Neither the evaluative nor the normative perspective is well suited to deal with these, caught up as those perspectives are in the disputes and realities of twenty years ago. We need to ask new questions in order to understand this new reality.

New research questions are now being asked. I will try to give some examples of the kind of questions I am talking about.

What is community?

In both the evaluative and normative perspectives the concept of 'community' has had a diffuse but largely undisputed meaning. However, as is often the case with undisputed assumptions, the idea of community has been simplified and somewhat romanticized. As more disabled people are being integrated, this taken-for-granted assumption about what constitutes community is being questioned.

One step in this direction – although not directly articulated as a critique of the community concept – was when Wolfensberger substituted the concept of normalization for that of social role valorization (Wolfensberger 1985). Instead of having 'the normal' or an abstract idea of 'community' as a point of reference, he builds on the realization that society is differentiated and that differentiation can be captured in terms of social roles. Making disabled people part of the community is thus just a first step. Being in that community means being part of the social structure, having social roles. In Wolfensberger's action-oriented theory the challenge then is to get mentally retarded people performing valued social roles.

From another angle, the concept of community has been questioned by feminist researchers. In an article with the telling title 'Whose "ordinary life" is it anyway?', two English researchers make the point that the community resources that are actually being mobilized are women, either as low-paid care workers or as unpaid carers of their own children (Brown and Smith 1989).

Other authors have stressed the fact that the idea of community in this context is a romantic one (Abraham 1989; Evans and Murcott 1990). Community is usually seen as consensus, belonging and equality. But we all know that this picture is only part of the truth. Society is also differentiated, stratified, an arena for conflicting interests, intolerance and discrimination. Living in the community therefore also means being confronted with these forces.

Another similar type of questioning of the community concept argues that community is seen too much as the sum of a number of autonomous and independent individuals (Cullen 1991). According to this critique, the community integration concept has a strong individualistic bias. A Norwegian sociologist (Waerness 1988) has argued that the ideal on which this ideology is built is the ideology of white middle-class men: men with no economic problems, who value their careers more than anything and are really not aware of their dependence on others, particularly women. What these critics are suggesting is that collective and communal aspects of society – our mutual dependence on each other – are neglected in much of the community integration rhetoric. A similar point has been made in the United States by Rud Turnbull, who argues for communitarian values as a substitute for the present emphasis on liberty-autonomy-independence regarding mental retardation (Turnbull 1991).

This discussion has so far been mostly conceptual, trying to find a better way of understanding what living in the community really means, by achieving a better understanding of what community is. I have no doubt that this will have important implications for empirical research in the future.

One such implication is that the point of reference can no longer – as in the evaluative and normative perspectives – be the segregated institution. Community living has to be interpreted in relation to society as such, not as some artificial substitution for what was. We have to start asking questions about the role and position of mentally retarded people in the societal structure, and stop judging their lives in relation to what it would have been like in an institution. No doubt they will sometimes be in positions and situations we do not like. But that can then be seen as a problem in itself, not, as is often the case today, as an argument in the debate about segregation–integration.

One step in that direction is the evaluative studies of deinstitutionalization and decentralization being carried out in Scandinavian countries (Kebbon et al. 1992; Tøssebro 1992). Data are indicators of people's standard of living that are routinely collected from a sample of the whole population. The idea, of course, is to relate a disabled person's situation to that of the rest of the population. This marks a shift from traditional research designs that would automatically consider a control group of other disabled people, probably those living in still existing institutions.

A similar broadening of research questions by questioning taken-for-granted assumptions can be found in research on the social relations of mentally retarded people living in the community and attitudes of non-disabled people towards disabilities.

Social relations

Many evaluative studies from several different countries show that physical integration does not necessarily mean that contacts within the community become established (Donnegan and Potts 1988; Zetlin and Murtaugh 1988). This has led some researchers to distinguish between physical integration – placement or physical location within the community – and social integration -- social inclusion within the community (Wolfensberger 1972). General findings show that school and housing integration in itself does not guarantee social integration. In an overview of school integration in Australia this is even referred to as 'social dumping' (Gow 1987). The social situation of those 'dumped' becomes worse, as they lack the contact and social support from their peers in special schools.

This has stimulated much research on the social relations of mentally retarded people placed within the community. In many studies voluntary, rewarding, mutual relations with non-disabled peers of the same age is the criterion for successful social integration, disregarding the fact that social relations are usually much more complicated and that integration in a social sense can hardly be restricted to such 'pure' forms of friendship relations. Furthermore, there has been a tendency to implicitly devalue other types of relations, such as those with other mentally retarded people.

In a recent book the Norwegian sociologist Jan Tøssebro (1992) discusses the social relations of people with moderate and severe mental retardation. He distinguishes between different types of relations according to how they are regulated. Friendship is a voluntary type of relationship characterized by spontaneity. Family relations on the other hand are normatively regulated. Family is not a question of choice but of strongly internalized social norms. A third type are the relations that start because people happen to be in the same place at the same time. Mentally retarded people have these kinds of relationships with similar people living in the same institution or group home. A fourth type of relation is the professional one, regulated by economic compensation for the person who is paid to work with a mentally retarded client.

One of Tøssebro's points is that the discussion of social integration so far has focused on friendship relations to the extent that other types of relations have been more or less forgotten. But if a mentally retarded person and his/her network are what is being studied, we naturally have to take all types of relations into account. Furthermore, the dividing line between different types of relations is not always that clear. Take, for example, the relation to paid staff. Several studies have reported that when mentally retarded people are asked who their best friend is, they often give the name of one of the personnel. This is usually interpreted as a negative sign and an indicator of how poor the social network of that person is. But many of us who have worked as staff know that this is not necessarily true. Quite often staff can develop a multifaceted relation with clients which extends to seeing each other in friend-like ways when off duty. This has also been shown empirically in a project in the United States by Taylor and Bogdan. They set out to investigate accepting and tolerant social relations between people with and without mental retardation. As opposed to sociology's emphasis on labelling, segregation and exclusion, they developed a programme called 'the sociology of acceptance' (Taylor and Bogdan 1989). One of the results of several qualitative studies within that programme is that many accepting friendship relations grew out of relations between staff and client or volunteers and client and that they sometimes are based on family linkage (Taylor and Bogdan 1989; Lutfiyya 1991).

Because relations with other mentally retarded people are often the result of being forced together, or being segregated, they have all too often been devalued as not really indicating social integration. But that does not mean that such relations cannot be of great value to the people involved and form an important and stable part of an individual person's network. Several studies of friendship relations between severely disabled persons have been reported. In some cases they are shown to have well developed and intimate friendship relations with each other, while other studies show that such relations with classmates in special classes and people living in the same group home or working in the same activity centre are practically non-existent, sometimes because these are discouraged by personnel (Clegg and Standen 1991; Gilkey and Zetlin 1987).

An English researcher, Dorothy Atkinson, has shown that continuity in relations is strongly related to positive adaptation when mentally retarded people move from an institution to community living. A friend from the institution or continued contact with the family can thus form the nucleus of a social network that can be developed within the community (Atkinson 1988; see also Day 1989).

What these results indicate is the importance of studying the social network of the mentally retarded in its own right. We should not restrict such studies to evaluating how well the social relations under study match up to our own image of what ideal community integration should be like; that is, seeing pure and ideal friendship relations as the only measure of successful integration.

Attitudes

The same simplification as is found in research on social relations is also shown in research on attitudes towards the mentally retarded. When problems in social relations, isolation or discrimination occur, there is a tendency to blame the attitudes of others. These are often postulated as being negative and prejudiced. Of course, prejudices do exist, but it is a simplification to view every social problem as a straightforward outgrowth of such attitudes. Attitudes are too complicated to be captured in a simple positive/negative or

prejudiced/non-prejudiced continuum. Research indicates that attitudes can best be understood as ambivalent, rather than as generally
negative or prejudiced (Lewis 1973; Söder 1990), and as strongly
dependent on the social context (Chadsey-Rush *et al.* 1989).

Neighbourhood opposition to group homes is a case in point.
American research suggests that as many as 25–35 per cent of group
homes have been subjected to opposition from neighbours. Studies
in England indicate roughly the same figures (Roycroft and Hames
1990). Such opposition is usually attributed to prejudice among
neighbours (Kastner and Repucci 1979).

But that interpretation can be questioned. In a study of attitudes
in Ireland, McConkey has shown that attitudes are not generally
negative. In a large survey it turned out that both people living close
to group homes and those who did not expressed rather favourable
attitudes. The worries they had about group homes mostly concerned the well-being of the residents. Almost a third of those living
close to a group home also declared that they wanted closer contact
with the residents of those homes (McConkey 1990).

In Sweden 13 per cent of existing group homes report having been
subject to opposition from neighbours. Gustavsson (1990) conducted intensive interviews with opposing neighbours, and his
interpretation of the reason for opposition was not based on prejudice. It can better be understood as an attempt by the protesters to
exert influence over their immediate neighbourhood. They are
protesting against authoritarian authorities more than against the
mentally retarded. Home and neighbourhood are arenas where
people feel the right to protect their privacy and autonomy. Some
would even argue that this protective feeling is growing as alienation
in other arenas, like work, politics and public affairs, is increasing.
What the protesting neighbours are doing can be seen as an expression of such trends in society generally and cannot be reduced
to expressions of negative attitudes towards disabled people
(Gustavsson 1990).

In other words, inequality and discrimination are facts of community life. Understanding their causes, expressions and implications for disabled people or the mentally retarded is a most important
task for research. In order to do that we have to state the questions
in such a way that we are not postulating that problems always relate
to the unwillingness, negative attitudes and prejudices of people
living within that community.

INTEGRATION IN SCHOOL

As was noted initially, the above discussion includes integration within education. My general point – that both the evaluative and the normative perspective have dominated to the extent that some relevant research questions have not been asked – is also valid here. But this general point, as shown in educational research, needs elaborating upon.

Education is a more delimited field than 'society' or 'community' in general. The school system is subject to political and/or bureaucratic control, while the education system is perceived to be more easily manipulated than 'society' and 'community'. Within education, integration is consequently often discussed on the premise that we are in control; both the education context and education practice are thought of as being controllable. We feel that we can, and should, manipulate it in order to achieve our goals.

As a result, the normative perspective (how do we achieve integration?) has probably been more present in education research than in integration research in general. The idea that integration is something we do for 'them' is more easily upheld, given that we feel responsibility and consider it possible to manipulate the school environment.

A dominant feature in research on school integration is that it is limited to integration within the school context. How integration in that context is related to integration in society or the community at large is often neglected, although not always totally absent.

Integration in the school context

Normative research that discusses integration within the school context has – more than other integration research – been caught up in what might be called the integration paradox: in order to integrate someone we have to assume that that someone is 'not integrated'. Referring to the process of integration builds on the assumption that somehow someone is in need of being brought (by 'us') into 'normal' life. In that sense integration presupposes some kind of segregation.

Much of the discussion in education research – and in particular in the normative research which tries to find ways of accomplishing 'true' integration – can be seen as attempts to overcome this inherent paradox. One expression of these attempts is the ambition to find 'better' terms like 'inclusion' or 'Regular Education Initiative'. But none of these new terms can overcome the paradox: viewing someone as in some way being 'special' or having 'special needs' is in itself a way of separating that person from what is considered 'normal'. No matter how great the ambition to overcome this basic separation, sooner or later this paradox leads us back to a discussion where integration (or whatever) is reduced to a rather technical discussion on 'how to do it' (Slee 1993b).

This technical way of treating integration also gets caught up in the simplified way of viewing attitudes and social relations as pointed out above. Attitudes are seen as obstacles. Teacher as well as peer attitudes have been studied over and over again from the standpoint that they constitute the main reason why attempts at social integration fail. Much in the same way as discussed generally above, the complexities of attitudes are reduced to a question of being positive or negative in relation to the goal of integration. Also in the same way as discussed above, social relations are evaluated in terms of spontaneous relations with non-disabled peers, most evidently in sociometric studies, where quantity of relations with non-disabled students is considered a valid measure of the degree of integration.

There are indications from qualitative studies in Scandinavia that the whole question of integration is seen in quite another light by people who have – fully or partly – been exposed to it. In a study of young adults with orthopaedic impairments, Solvang (1994) shows that those who have been attending special high schools are usually satisfied with that experience, especially with the network of peers with disabilities into which they were integrated. Those who have been fully integrated on the other hand were very critical about segregated schools. Solvang's interpretation is that this mirrors a stereotype about segregated education that these young people have internalized but never really experienced.

In a study in Sweden – also with youngsters with orthopaedic disabilities – Barron (1995) points out that her informants usually had a rather pragmatic opinion when discussing their school experience. Some had been for several years in special classes, though they were not generally dissatisfied with that. On the contrary, those who were in special classes during high school described it as a rewarding experience. More generally, Barron notes that the issue of integration–segregation does not seem to be at the core of their criticism. It was, rather, questions related to autonomy, peer relations and future support services when moving away from home that were at the top of their agenda.

In order to ask new questions about integration within the school context we thus have to move away from the normative and rather technical way of viewing the school situation of pupils with disabilities in terms of successful integration or not. Research that focuses on the experiences of pupils with disabilities seems to be a more fruitful way of doing that.

School integration within a societal context

Studies of school integration have generally focused on the school context. But the school is an institution within society. If we are to understand what goes on in school as well as the effects of that in later life, we have to view school and education in a societal context.

One type of empirical study that does link school and special education to society is the traditional follow-up one. Historically, these studies have had quite an impact, not least in showing that pupils with disabilities are capable of living self-sufficient lives and of contributing to society. A classical study by Fernald (1919) became a milestone in showing that all the retrospective studies of degenerative families were wrong. In a follow-up study he was able to show that a substantial number of people leaving school institutions were capable of living autonomously in society. Later follow-up studies have usually shown basically the same picture. One problem faced by these studies – not unlike the criteria problem in other evaluative studies discussed above – is the difficulty in finding meaningful and reliable outcome measures. 'Adaptation' is much too vague and complex a process to be captured by single measures (Edgerton 1984). More information is often gained by using qualitative studies (Edgerton 1967) or a combination of quantitative and qualitative data (e.g., Richardson *et al.* 1988).

While traditional follow-up studies have usually worked within the research tradition we call evaluative, the follow-up studies of integration have had a much more normative approach. Typically they have been couched as studies of transition from school to adult life, thus taking an instrumental and normative perspective on the whole question of what happens to youngsters with disabilities after school. From a transition perspective schools have been criticized for not providing training opportunities that facilitate access to the labour market. The normative approach has resulted in attempts to define what a worthy adult life should be like, resulting in lists of individual characteristics for fulfilling the adult role (Blalock 1988; OECD 1991).

But by taking this normative approach, some of the interesting questions concerning what happens to pupils with disabilities who have been integrated within school become obscured. The whole concept of transition grows out of the same normative assumptions – the same ideals about normality – as integration. Future research which aims to broaden the research questions will probably have to return to the more empirically based follow-up studies, but without getting caught up in the criteria dilemma.

One way of doing this is to put the question of integration into a broader ideological perspective, taking the integration paradox described above seriously. This would mean taking a step backwards and – instead of asking the technical 'how questions' about integration – asking questions about the exclusion that forms the basis for the whole integration discourse (Fulcher 1989b). Such a perspective can relate to the writings of some British sociologists who take a critical view of education in general and special education in particular (Barton and Tomlinson 1984; Tomlinson 1982). By emphasizing both how schools reproduce inequalities in society and the role of special education and special education professionals within it, the question of what goes on within the school context is viewed in a different light. In that light both the evaluative and the normative perspective on integration stand out as rather limited and ideologically naive.

BEYOND EFFECT AND HOW-TO-DO-IT

As community integration has developed, much useful and important research has been done on its effects and on how to promote it. But in order to understand the normalized and integrated lives of people with disabilities living within the community we have to start asking other questions than those about effect and success.

We have to see the situation of people with disabilities in relation to the society they live in. We should start asking questions in which their lives are the central focus of our studies, not in order to evaluate or change them, but primarily to understand them. Such research questions are being asked today. I have pointed to some areas where this is taking place.

In education research there seem to be two promising lines of research that can contribute to such a development. The first one aims at understanding what goes on in the school context in a new light. Qualitative studies with inductive and ethnographic ambitions can help us understand social patterns and subjective experiences in terms other than as effects of integration. The second line relates to the broader societal context, where a return to the empirical follow-up studies informed by critical questions about exclusion and segregation can help us transcend the narrow and technical questions about effect and how-to-do-it.

Chapter 4

Beyond schooling

Integration in a policy perspective

Gunnar Stangvik

INTRODUCTION

The concept of integration has continuously gained currency in Norway. From being regarded as a specific way of solving the problems of pupils with disabilities in traditional schooling, it has become a basic principle for educating them to become valued and participating members of society. This orientation has put the social philosophy of regular and special education on our agenda – a fact that has demanded that more attention be paid to social development. This orientation has had an important impact on how to interpret integration issues. Integration is not a goal in itself, but a principle and a means of achieving long-term social goals of education.

Important questions to ask in this perspective are:

1 How should the concept of integration be defined? Is it only an educational construct related to schooling, or does it also indicate a new social policy regarding disabilities and handicaps? This question is important because the answer defines the theoretical scope of the construct and the types of action considered necessary.

2 What is the goal of integration? This relates to the preceding question. However, the question here is whether integration should be restricted to conditions of schooling, or whether it also concerns inclusion in society.

3 What should be the role of special education? How should a role for special education be defined so that it is a partner of integration rather than an enemy?

4 What competencies are needed? Competency is a complex of skills and values which cannot be separated. The question is, to what

extent does a new set of values have to be adopted and interiorized by professionals in order to become change agents for integration?
5 What are the most important integration imperatives? In order to implement this new policy a number of new behaviours and relationships have to be developed, some of which are quite alien to the traditional school system.

RESOURCES FOR TEACHERS

Clarifying goals and definitions

The question of resources needed for integration cannot be properly answered without defining the concept of integration, the goals to be achieved and the characteristics of the target groups. These are factors which will shape perceptions of what activities are needed in order to foster integration. The school perspective is only one of several perspectives.

Vislie (1995) and Stangvik (1994) discuss antecedents of the integration policy. Integration policy is regarded as a response to changes in the structure of the welfare state which have laid a new basis for a general welfare policy as well as for changes particularly relevant to the concept of handicap (see figure 4.1). Vislie and Stangvik regard integration as an emerging policy in a welfare state and an extension of one of its basic principles of managing deviancy.

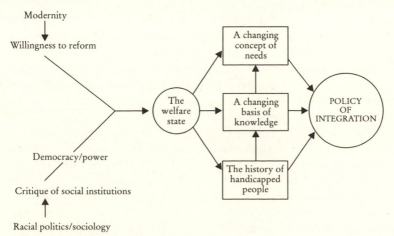

Figure 4.1 Integration policy: the background

Educational policy is only one aspect which has to be related to policies.

When the complex relationships indicated are taken into account, integration should not be thought of as a result of piecemeal social engineering, but as a general restructuring of the managing of disability and handicap. Such restructuring is a response to structural changes of the modern welfare state and to a new understanding of the living conditions and prospects of learning disabled. Hence, integration has to do with changing conditions of schooling and educating disabled people in a modern society.

This broad approach to integration underscores the need to clarify goals and objectives. Some of the questions which ought to be raised are: is integration only a matter of a new school organization – an attempt to implement a more rational and economic school system – or is it an educational question and a means to achieve a set of new objectives in schooling? If the latter is the case, what are these objectives? Is integration a means to achieve social inclusion for special needs pupils in all areas of society, or is the philosophy of integration only restricted to schooling? There is no single answer to these questions, but they ought to be properly addressed. Stangvik (1994) discusses a conceptual model of social inclusion (i.e., normalization) in which integration is but one of four theoretical dimensions. He applies integration to all relevant areas of life and shows that its implementation in different domains (including education) depends on activities at several levels (i.e., individual; family; agency; community; municipality; and state). Analysis indicates that the concept of integration should be understood at different paradigmatic levels, each level focusing on a different set of antecedents and consequences. Analytically, it seems necessary to distinguish between an individual-oriented, a social-oriented, a system-oriented and a society-oriented paradigm. Each of these adds a different dimension to the process of integration. Focusing on social interaction makes it necessary to pay attention to value clarification; focusing on the school system makes it necessary to focus on dysfunctional aspects of this system, while focusing on society makes it necessary to pay attention to conflicts between policy rhetoric and reality. This broad conceptual approach is needed in order to consider all facets of integration, and to underscore the fact that integration is not only a process of creating a new learning arrangement for individual children, but is concerned with innovation and change.

Focusing on the individual draws attention to individual conditions for integration and to individual results of the process. Söder (1980) distinguishes between physical, social, functional and societal integration. These definitions also indicate different levels of ambition of policy. Furthermore, ambitions have to be modified by the characteristics of the target groups of an integration policy. Learning disabilities seldom have a pure form. Really they are accompanied by hearing loss, sight problems, movement difficulties, problems of perception and co-ordination, behaviour problems and so on. In our country integration means, at least rhetorically, that the regular school system becomes responsible for catering for this pool of pupils. The challenge for integration policy is to organize all available education resources in a way that matches both the learning and developmental characteristics of the pupils as well as the goals of teaching under conditions of integration.

Responding to the problem

Theory and observations concerning the everyday world of the disabled show that integration requires a process of innovation and change. New resources are necessary as well as the reallocation of existing resources. Instead of being allocated to a segregated school setting, resources must now be reallocated to integrated settings. In a democratic society this cannot be done using a top-down model of change based on laws, rules and regulations. These are instruments which have to be used in accordance with professional preference and opinion. Depending on our definition, integration may have to do with changes of values, organization, didactics, methods, etc. These changes are not only personal matters, but relate to a whole matrix of circumstances.

Different ways of organizing resources are often thought of in terms of an integration scale ranging from the most restrictive to the least restrictive integration arrangement. Integration may then be defined as a specific way of organizing resources for teaching pupils with learning difficulties. In this way integration may be treated as a placement problem of no real implication for the regular school system. It seems to me that this phase of organizational reification has been ideologically passed in our country, where integration was redefined into a number of so-called special education arrangements. One reason for this is that in the 1980s, partly due to the impact of the concepts of normalization and inclusion, the concept of integration was developed and expanded. These concepts focused on the social development of children and made it clear that integration in schools was a means of achieving normal and valued roles in society. The integration debate acquired a new momentum, while research and evaluation of integration discovered new criteria and perspectives.

New ways of thinking assisted by a tide of decentralization have brought about the collapse of institutionalized provision, resulting in the dismantling of our special school system and relocating the mentally retarded to their home communities again. The demand for a broader concept of regular education is bound to follow in the wake of this process.

Rational resource planning for integration is therefore impossible without stating explicitly what the goals are. I have tried to show that integration goals may vary considerably in depth and scope. Integration also has to be based on research about the social and psychological situation of pupils with special needs and knowledge about the most important factors for achieving such short- and long-term integration goals. This very basic logic is shown by figure 4.2.

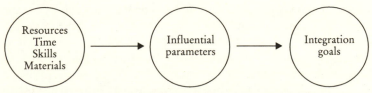

Figure 4.2 Integration: the relation between means and goals

Previous research (cf. Stangvik 1979) tends to show that the question of teaching resources cannot be separated from the existential world of the learner. Self-evaluation is one important aspect of this world, which is strongly related to the social aspects of the school setting -- i.e. to integration.

From the point of view of change, the question of resources is only one aspect of the change process. Resources are mediated by people. Experiences from our own country show that becoming a professional mediator of integration is an incremental process which takes time. This process consists of several stages: from open to hidden resistance through passive acceptance, while today we are on the verge of active acceptance. It has taken us approximately twenty years. This process clearly shows that political reform strategies have to include strategies for value clarification. The depth of reform strategies depends on the definition of integration on which integration policy is based.

EDUCATIONAL ORGANIZATION

Planning for integration in schooling

According to the principle of integration, a comprehensive and non-segregatory model of education is preferred. However, in schools a bi-modal approach to teaching has been adopted which treats specific needs of pupils as something that is extracurricular to regular teaching. Hence, a (re)allocation of educational resources is needed which makes the school organization more compatible with the principle of integration. In order to do so, certain questions regarding educational services for these pupils need to be raised.

The first one relates to the philosophy of education and could be formulated as follows: is the selected service model compatible with the ideology of integration? In order to answer this question, each of the educational alternatives may be understood as micro-climates characterized by a specific setting, activity patterns, ways of grouping pupils and types of communication, and all alternatives may be thought of in terms of a service continuum which may be arranged along a scale from the least to the most restrictive, with reference to a normal classroom setting, i.e. integration. This is one important approach to policy analyses of educational alternatives for integration. This approach has been described by Flynn and Nitsch (1980), Solum and Stangvik (1993) and Stangvik (1993, 1994). It is an important strategy for evaluation and for monitoring the process of integration in schools.

According to the principle of integration, educational placement should be non-categorical, demanding that the educational context should match the characteristics of the individual child. Hence, the second question is empirical and could be formulated as follows: which alternative in the continuum of educational alternatives is most effective in order to attain the integration goals for this particular individual?

In order to answer this question careful individual evaluation is needed. This evaluation differs from a traditional one in that it should be directly connected to long-term educational planning for the child. The placement decision, which may be one result of the evaluation, should be seen as transient and be constantly revised in order to support the pupil in mastering a less restrictive alternative. Such mastery of course also depends on factors related to the environmental setting. Hence, the educational organization should always be in focus.

New knowledge and skills are needed

Integration policy means a new school agenda. It changes the focus of teaching and requires other formulations of problems and needs than special school teaching. The special school code is different from the regular class code, making knowledge and skills less transferable between settings. They have to be reformulated in terms of a new set of values and applied to a very different context. Therefore, a programme of re-education is needed.

In our country, there seems to have been no active professional relations between the special school system and the regular one. This may be due partly to long distances between special schools and pupils' home communities. In spite of some twenty years of state integration policy, research tends to show few systematic attempts by special schools to reintegrate their pupils into their home communities. However, new reforms have placed this reintegration on the top of the special school agenda.

Norway is presently dismantling its special school system and turning a number of special schools into competency centres. This is part of a programme for restructuring special education and making it more compatible with policies of integration and normalization. As a part of this process, a competency programme for special school personnel has been launched.

Experience of this reform process indicates that professionals tend to preserve segregated practices. How this comes about may perhaps be understood by realizing that integration implies decentralization of power and control to communities, local schools and regular classrooms. This calls for a redefinition of roles. Presently the special school system is ascribed the role of a service partner to the regular class and to the community. As pointed out, resources have been made available for re-educating special school personnel. One problem, however, is that re-education is provided by educational institutions which base their education on traditional roles and provide few opportunities for practising role behaviours needed for teaching in integrated settings.

The core message here is that the first stage of an innovation process – the value clarification and conceptualization stage – ought to be taken seriously. If not, resources will continue to be allocated in accordance with traditional preferences. This is a dilemma of a decentralized system. Integration becomes a matter of choice, making integration dependent upon the integration discourse being kept alive by professionals.

Competing integration discourses

The actual policy is a result of negotiation between ideology and reality. State sanction of an integration ideology is of restricted importance in a decentralized society. In a complex social reality an integration policy instigates several competing discourses. For teachers, integration may be thought of in terms of the stress it puts on classroom teaching, lack of traditional placement alternatives, and so on; for school administrators integration may be a matter of new ways of budgeting; for parents the experienced short-term effects and the assumed long-term effects of integration on their children may be the focus.

All these discourses may be regarded as expressions of different interest groups which have differing power and control over the integration process. In a decentralized system there is no safe way to assure that one discourse is ascribed primacy. Hence, it seems consistent with reality to describe the actual concept and the principle of integration as negotiated social products of these competing discourses. Results from a competency training project on integration and inclusion indicated that participants were not sufficiently able to define these concepts socially in spite of the fact that they are the basic starting-points of two ongoing state reforms (Stangvik and Simonsen 1993).

Decentralization, flexibility and decision-making power

True integration means that placement decisions become less important and that more attention is paid to practical educational decisions concerning schooling. It puts the social development of the individual in focus. This means a number of here-and-now questions of integration have to be solved at the grass-roots level by the people closest to that person. Expanding the concept of integration to pupils in need of care in the school situation makes it necessary for the school to consider itself as a part, and only as one part, of the child's ecological social system.

This calls for a redistribution of power and control of education. Decisions should be based on active communication between key parties in the social environment of the child in order to ensure that integration has ecological validity, i.e. integration should have meaning outside the auspices of the school. This adaptation of schooling to the individual child in a particular social context ultimately calls for decentralization, flexibility and authorization to use resources according to individual plans. But, as already indicated, such a bottom-up model of integration is associated with certain risks: professional preferences may define what is considered to be best for the child instead of a rational analysis of the child's life situation and the goals of integration. How to keep the integration discourse alive is one of the intricate problems of a decentralized system.

Co-operation

Co-operation is basic to integrating special needs pupils. However, the types of co-operation needed depend on target groups and the aims of an integration policy. Co-operation should not be restricted to co-operation between schools if the aim is to foster long-term social development towards participation and valued social roles for children with a variety of specific needs.

A co-operative model has to be established which ensures that:

1 the regular school system has access to all available knowledge and competence for educating special needs pupils;
2 the aims of integration are kept constantly alive in planning and teaching;
3 teaching and education are adapted to the child's particular situation.

The last point implies that the concept of co-operation cannot be based solely on school expertise, but also has to include persons relevant to the child's 'private life'. Hence it is necessary to build a competency network around individual children. A first-line operational team is required to solve the day-to-day problems of integrated teaching in the school context, while a second-line body of experts needs to be available for the different types of specific needs. In Norway experts who may be called upon are usually located both at the local level (pedagogical-psychological services), the regional level (speech and hearing therapists, regional competency centres), as well as at the state level (state competency centres).

In our experience this diversity of people has very different discourses and results in attempts to create very different agendas, some of which may actually run contrary to integration policy. Therefore, there is obviously a need for a working model which helps to ensure that the competency network co-ordinates activities according to a set of common goals. These goals should be made operational by means of criteria and instruments for planning and evaluation (cf. Stangvik 1994). However, it is abundantly clear that such a person-oriented model of integrated education for pupils with special needs will be incompatible with the code of traditional regular schooling with its whole-class instruction, 40- to 45-minute teaching periods, subject teaching and so on. Therefore, the actual integration of pupils will have to be a negotiated social product which is ultimately a question of what is possible within specific educational, social, cultural and political boundaries. These boundaries cannot be defined by state policy. To lay a basis for a comprehensive education, including pupils with special needs, is a step-wise process in which the person-oriented model of special education has to be corroborated into a model of change and innovation of regular schooling.

CHANGING SCHOOLS IN ORDER TO IMPROVE INTEGRATION

Making the school more comprehensive

The principle of integration demands that schools are made more comprehensive in order to cater for a broad variety of pupils. However, the rational use of resources in order to make regular education more comprehensive is heavily restricted by the way things work in schools. The result of this is that in order to match schooling to the actual differences between learners, one has to rely increasingly on special education, and little by little integration is thought of as a specific placement alternative in a continuum of special education alternatives. Seen as an individualized concept of special education, the concept of integration loses its momentum and represents no challenge to traditional teaching. Thus it is important to uncover the role of special education in the process of integration.

Time frames, teaching periods, teacher role differentiation, number of pupils in classes, ability composition, architecture, curricula and so on, serve to determine communication behaviour and how time is used in classrooms. This has been a prominent theme in Swedish educational research, showing relationships between such frame factors and time used at different intellectual levels of the school subjects and between frame factors and classroom communication (cf. Lundgren 1972). These factors create a restricted code of teaching. What is needed in order to implement integration in school is an elaborated code.

In order to change the somewhat ritualistic patterns of classroom teaching that make it difficult to cater for pupil differences, classes should be subdivided for a greater part of the school day than is the case today, and more of the curriculum should be frequently organized into projects providing greater opportunities for learning experiences than traditional subject teaching.

Several strategies for reforming regular education so that teaching adapts more to needs and differences have been tried:

- Additional resources have been used to divide classes. This has allowed more time for individual teaching, but there is no sign of any radical change of classroom practices.
- Additional resources have been used for a second teacher in the classroom or for assistants. Studies of the work of itinerant co-teachers show that they mostly work to smooth the clockwork of the traditional school model. Furthermore, studies of assistants for pre-school children with disabilities tend to show that they structure interaction in ways that diminish contact with other pupils in the classroom.
- Teachers have been given special training, which is frequently based on the traditional school model. In fact, the training model seems to be symmetrical to a segregated and categorized special education system, and far less oriented towards solving educational needs in a regular school setting.
- Vast resources are used for educational and psychological provision for teachers and classrooms. However, these provisions are too often oriented towards placement decisions rather than contributing to the educational programme of the individual child.

The role of special education

In spite of all this there is still a strong and indefinite demand for special education outside regular classrooms. Paradoxically, this segregated model of teaching may be regarded as an expression of the principle of integration – if not at classroom level, then at least at school level. Due to this kind of special education pupils with special needs have been able to stay within their classes in regular schools on a part-time basis. Statistics from Norway (Vislie 1995) show that most pupils with special needs (84 per cent) are catered for in regular schools and classes. Under the present conditions of schooling it seems safe to conclude that special education has been an important factor in keeping many pupils with special needs in a regular setting. However, such a criterion of integration is too conservative. If integration is defined socially and functionally the picture changes. It is also a fact that huge resources are spent on special education models which segregate children from mainstream education either in special classes, or in groups of varying stability for varying amounts of time. In order to solve such conflicts special education competence has to be severed from its present organizational alternatives and made part of regular education. It is necessary to create a change agency. How that can be done is a question of the utmost importance.

According to Vislie (1995), two strategies have been attempted: focus has been put on special education, 'i.e. integration is mainly seen as a reform in special education' (13), or focus has been on the general education system, 'i.e. the major concerns being related to reformation of regular education, to make it more comprehensive' (13). This seems to be a conceptual dichotomy relevant to a discussion of resources. However, it seems that the concept 'comprehensive' in the Scandinavian context is a political-educational one which has mainly been part of a social policy giving equal rights to schooling to all social classes in society and to a lesser extent is aimed at giving these rights to persons with special needs. In fact, the discussion of this group was not a central element in the debate on comprehensive education, and regular and segregated special education have simultaneously been developed. In fact, the most rapid development of special education took place in the 1960s and 1970s, in those years when comprehensive education was being implemented.

The implementation of integration

Implementing integration is a question of innovation and we could profit much from learning about the relevant stages in adopting an innovation. According to Flynn and Nitsch (1980) adoption-in-theory is primary; it can be divided into different stages:

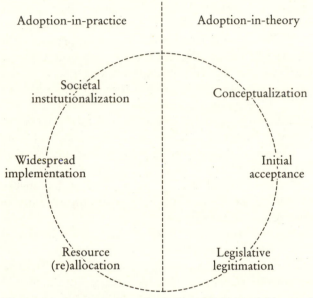

Adoption-in-practice | Adoption-in-theory

Societal institutionalization

Conceptualization

Widespread implementation

Initial acceptance

Resource (re)allocation

Legislative legitimation

Figure 4.3 Stages in the adoption cycle of a social innovation
Source: Flynn and Nitsch 1980: 364

How integration is conceptualized is perceived to be of primary importance. However, change is not only a question of cognition. Acceptance plays a fundamental role in the change process in order to ensure legislation and resources. Acceptance has to do with values. Focusing on acceptance underscores the need for value clarification by the change agents.

Based on the preceding points, one may safely conclude that the question of resources should be evaluated with respect to a thorough analysis of the concept of integration. If not, additional resources will tend to be used to maintain a traditional system. However, such system maintenance may be skilfully covered by integration rhetoric.

According to the stages in this change cycle, a number of strategies are needed in order to implement integration:

- Re-education: professionals have to be given every opportunity to adopt values, concepts and methods which are conducive to integration.

- Evaluation: professionals have to be constantly engaged in evaluation activities based on criteria of integration.
- Development of new working methods: the social-developmental focus of integration demands a new education direction. The goal is not only to produce a state of social equilibrium in regular classes with pupils with special needs, but to foster these children's participation, competency development and independence (Stangvik 1994) in the short and long term. This perspective has many consequences for selecting content, organizing educational work and teaching methods.
- Organizational development: the social-developmental focus of integration has to be kept in mind all the time by those involved in the education process, and should be the basis of all planning for the child. The objectives of this are to organize all available resources according to the goals of integration, and to monitor the integration of individual pupils in school and society. In order to achieve the first objective, multilevel organization is required, and in order to achieve the second organization has to evolve around the individual child. Hence, a multidisciplinary organizational interface is needed.

EXTERNAL FACTORS

Prevailing public opinion

As pointed out earlier, integration initiates a number of discourses. Prevailing public opinion on integration is an elusive construct, but it may be thought of as the dominant discourse in a particular society at a particular point in time. Integration has to do with managing persons with specific needs. The study of history shows that the prevailing opinion of handicapped people has been formed by the modality of thinking in particular periods, and that they have been ascribed different roles. Hence public opinion should not be reified, but ought to be considered as a social construct related to cultural conditions as defined by ideologists and science, as well as to the actual living conditions.

The type of public opinion able to set the political agenda depends on its power base. As far as integration is concerned, a prevailing public opinion is difficult to discern in the political debate. One reason for this is that the concept of integration has become esoteric, particularistic and technical, and is perceived by most people as something that has only to do with schooling. In order to break this vicious circle and to create a true public debate which may reveal the prevailing public opinion, the concept of integration has to be replaced with concepts like participation, co-operation, equality and valued roles. If this cannot be done the integration agenda will be set by prevailing professional opinion – more precisely, the most powerful part of it.

The role of the media

The media play an important part in forming opinion in modern society, which is clearly shown in the integration debate. In order to realize the impact of the media it is necessary to see how it works. First there is the principle of particularization. Reforms like integration are based upon values which give priority to continuity and wholeness in the educational process. In order to preserve these basic features of the concept of integration a public debate is needed which allows room for the complexity of the issue. To be manageable to the press the concept of integration is deconstructed into isolated elements which have the character of news and are presented in short texts and big pictures. Second, material has to be personalized, i.e. complex issues like social reforms have to be made flesh and blood. Third, there is the principle of the polarizing headline, i.e. in order to sell, information has to be compressed into a short headline and ascribed a negative value.

In this way the media easily become a conservative force in the process of social change, instead of the critical force they purport to be. Thus it is almost impossible for modern media to act as mediators regarding the background narrative to integration policy. At least this seems to be the case in contemporary Norway. The facts about the effects of reforms are continually distorted by the media. Among other things, this is particularly evident when research on the effects of reforms on consumers is compared with how the same reforms are featured in the press. Overall, this process shows the need for empirical research which is able to act as a corrective when the agenda of public opinion is set.

Teacher opinion

Two aspects related to teacher opinion should be considered: teachers carry the 'burden' of integration and teachers are 'public servants'.

The foregoing means that teachers are trapped between loyalty to policy and the realities of everyday life in the classroom. In Norway and Sweden special education took a lot of the heat out of the situation. As pointed out earlier, special education expanded rapidly when comprehensive education was introduced. Special education became an adjunct to regular education. This measure had at least two functions: first, it preserved the traditional class model of teaching in regular classes and served to pacify teacher opinion on integration. Second, this type of special education preserved an integration rhetoric. Regular class teachers have not yet been put to any strong test concerning their opinion on integration. This will come when integration policy becomes a policy of change for regular class teaching aimed at creating a school for all children.

However, schools are responsive to society and the dominant model of teaching may be thought of as a natural product of negotiation between the physical, ideological and economic frameworks of schooling. The model for schooling may be described in terms of how time is used, in terms of the relationship between students and teachers, and in terms of content. It seems reasonable to assume that teachers' mentality is structured by demands for 'survival' in these micro-environments. From this point of view it seems unlikely that teachers will favour a policy of integration which does not focus on their need for support and assistance in the classroom.

Many teachers do not feel that integration is their problem. They perceive integration to be a political and administrative problem which should be met by physical measures. Teachers may feel that pupils do not belong in their classroom because they are considered not to benefit from the dominant ways of teaching in regular classes, and they may also be considered to stand in the way of this teaching. Pupils who do not profit from traditional teaching may then be considered unfit for attending regular classes. Therefore, in order to implement an integration policy, both a change of values and a change of organization are needed. Our experience clearly shows that it is not sufficient to add new resources to the present system. There will probably be no limit to the need for new resources. There seems to be no easy way out: greater priority needs to be given to the social goals of teaching, and the principle of individualization has to be vested with practical meaning.

CONCLUSION

Teaching is heavily dependent on values, traditions and existing organizational frameworks and cannot be understood solely in terms of the resources available to teachers. Consequently, all these aspects have to be kept in view in order to understand the prospects for integration in a particular society. Integration should therefore be thought of in terms of change and innovation related to organizational development, value clarification, and creating new learning environments.

The level of change necessary to implement integration depends on the scope of the definition. I have attempted to show that the concept of integration ought to be understood at different paradigmatic levels, from an individual-oriented paradigm of integration to a society-oriented paradigm. Each of these paradigms focuses on a different set of implementation parameters. Discussing the role of special education, I have tried to show that integrating individual children cannot be solved on the basis of an individual-oriented paradigm.

The implications of a special education model of integration which allocates the bulk of resources to education provision outside classrooms are different from those of a truly comprehensive model which allocates resources for special education to regular classrooms. Expanding the integration concept to encompass societal inclusion would also widen its scope. This sufficiently underscores the need for a change and an innovation model of integration.

The regular classroom is an important battleground for achieving integration. However, allocating resources to regular classrooms is not sufficient. Time, skills and materials have to be used in ways which are compatible with the broader goals of integration. In order to do this, a developmental perspective is needed which makes it possible to apply the concept to the individual child. This perspective is necessary in order to organize educational content in terms of short-term and long-term goals. Long-term goals of integration cannot be successfully achieved only by adjusting the norms and methods of traditional classrooms. Work in the classroom ought to be understood as a means of supporting successful integration into society; this is the inclusion perspective.

Individual educational plans are needed which restructure resources in terms of long-term integration goals. Long-term integration cannot be achieved by compensatory strategies, or by other models which keep the goals and objectives of teaching unchanged. At least, it cannot be achieved by such methods without restricting the integration policy to pupils with specific learning disabilities, i.e. children with no physical, mental or behavioural deficits beside their learning difficulties. This would of course restrict the implications of an integration policy. Hence, it is important to decide the target groups of an integration policy.

There are a variety of pupils with special needs available for an integrated setting; pupils with varying needs of adaptation of their learning environment. Some of them may need only small changes made to their learning environment, others need radical changes. The challenge is to define a practical integration policy in accordance with the specific needs and the available educational contexts.

Education should prepare pupils for future social roles and should be thought of as a means of including pupils with special needs in society. The concept signifies the school counterpart of a general inclusion-oriented social policy and a means of implementing such a general policy in public schooling. Societal integration is the long-term goal. Such a goal has several implications for schooling as regards its organization and selection of teaching methods and content.

Officially, special education has become an administrative and legal concept in Norway, defining educational activities outside the regular classroom. Special education is contrasted to 'adaptive teaching' (*tilpasset opplaering*) which has to do with adaptive arrangements in regular classrooms. This distinction has little to do with a professional concept of special education, but seems to represent attempts to defend the state purse against unjustified claims in court from citizens who are ready to test their rights to special education. In reality, it reinforces a bi-modal approach to educational organization which underscores the fact that pupils with special needs do not belong in the mainstream. What is needed is a concept of special education which defines it in terms of arranging effective teaching for individuals with specific needs, independent of settings, and which takes as its starting-point the least restrictive setting as the preferable one.

Competency is related to values. Integration is based on a specific set of values, which decide what is considered important, relevant, correct and justifiable in the education process. Hence it is difficult to transmit knowledge and skills between systems based on different sets of values. In order to become a change agent for integration, the concept of integration has to be adopted at a mental level to the extent that it becomes an integral part of a professional role. Integration has to be seen as the professionally preferable alternative. This demands a re-education process which makes value clarification a part of this process. Such re-education has increased prominence in democratic societies where 'bottom-up' models of change are the only viable alternatives.

Integration depends on individual long-term planning and education. In order to plan and to educate effectively, education has to be a co-operative project between people who have sufficient insight into the school and a person's life situation. Hence, a redistribution of power and control of education is needed. The traditional school setting is only one part of the education of the child. In order to define what is best for the child, participation in the process of schooling is needed. The ultimate challenge for the integration-oriented school system is to implement individual plans within the context of regular schooling. In order to do so, integration has also to be defined in terms of change and innovation in schooling and society.

In order to implement integration fully, schools have to change. This change is impossible without a new ideology. Hence, it cannot be achieved by organizational development alone. Such development has to be supported by re-education. Prevailing public opinion, including the opinion of teachers, is a product of history and present circumstances. Trapped between the Scylla of the new ideology and the Charybdis of present classroom realities, teachers search for new solutions. Both aspects ought to be considered seriously.

Chapter 5

The reform of special education or the transformation of mainstream schools?

Alan Dyson and Alan Millward

INTRODUCTION

This chapter examines the question of how national governments can promote the integration of children with special needs into mainstream (regular) schools. It argues that although it is tempting to see integration as a reform of special education, its success actually depends upon the transformation of mainstream schools in ways which make them more able to respond to the diversity of student characteristics. This transformation itself depends upon a paradigm shift at a number of levels within education – not least in the way school managers and class teachers conceptualize their approach to student diversity. Paradigm shifts of this sort cannot simply be legislated into being, and therefore governments have to find sophisticated means of managing change.

UNDERSTANDING INTEGRATION

Integration is a deceptive and slippery concept. On the face of it, nothing could be simpler than the idea that children should be placed in mainstream (regular) schools rather than in special schools. It is, at least superficially, a process which can be managed through national legislation and supported through the deployment of central resources. In other words, it is an ideal arena for centralized reform. We wish to suggest, however, that integration, properly understood, is far from simple; that the relationship between the inclusion of children with special needs in mainstream schools and the process of central legislation and reform is complex and tenuous; and that sophisticated forms of change-management are necessary if integration that is meaningful is to result.

We shall begin by defining our own understanding of integration:

Integration is not about the relocation of pupils from special to mainstream schools, nor is it about finding ways of replicating special forms of provision within the mainstream. Rather, it is about reforming mainstream schools in ways which make them more responsive to the individual differences of the children within them. And the successful achievement of this reform depends on paradigmatic shifts, not simply at the level of policy and structure, but also at the level of the constructions of special needs undertaken by particular teachers in particular schools.

This understanding starts from a distinction made by Lise Vislie (1995) between two fundamentally different ways in which Western countries have approached the issue of integration over the past two decades. On the one hand, Vislie argues, there are countries which have seen integration essentially as a reform of their special education system. The aim of reform has been to find ways of extending special education programmes and services into mainstream (regular) schools. This approach, Vislie suggests, is characteristic of countries such as Germany, England and Belgium. On the other hand, there are countries which have understood the movement towards integration as a reform of mainstream education; that is, they have sought ways of making mainstream schools more responsive to the particular characteristics of children with special educational needs. Such countries would include Denmark, Sweden, Norway and the United States.

Vislie argues that outcomes from the former group of countries have been somewhat disappointing; a great deal of activity and apparent change has not in fact substantially increased the proportion of children placed in genuinely integrated settings. It is the latter group of countries – those which have focused on the reform of mainstream schools – that have been the more successful in promoting forms of integration that are more than merely nominal. We wish to support and elaborate Vislie's argument in order to understand why it should be that reform of mainstream schools proves to be the more effective approach to integration, and to understand more fully what that reform might look like. In so doing, we will draw upon a series of investigations we have undertaken into innovations in special needs provision in mainstream schools in the United Kingdom (Clark *et al.* 1995a, 1995b; Dyson 1992; Dyson *et al.* 1994).

COMPETING PARADIGMS

The key concepts in the field of special education – 'disability', 'handicap', 'special educational needs', 'learning difficulty', and so on – are by no means unproblematic. It is becoming increasingly obvious that, far from being self-evident descriptions of children's 'objective' characteristics, they are constructions which emerge in particular times and places, and which may be seen to serve certain social interests (Barton and Oliver 1992; Fulcher 1989a; Oliver 1990; Slee 1993a; Tomlinson 1982). These constructions in turn are founded upon paradigmatic ways of viewing the differences between people in general and children in particular.

Two such paradigms have been identified (Ainscow 1994; Halliwell and Williams 1993) as being in competition within the field of special education. The first is the 'psycho-medical' paradigm (Clark *et al.* 1995a) or the 'individual gaze' (Fulcher 1989a). This paradigm understands special needs (or disability, or whatever term is in use) as intelligible entirely or largely in terms of the characteristics of the 'disabled' individual. It is these characteristics which are seen to account for the inability of certain children to flourish within the provision made in mainstream education. It follows that the appropriate educational response to these characteristics is either to change them through some form of remedial intervention, or to make alternative provision for the child in the form of an adapted (often reduced) curriculum, delivered in the context of special forms of support and teaching, and very possibly within a 'special' setting. It is this paradigm, of course, which informs the whole apparatus of special education as it has developed in contemporary Western education systems.

Alongside this psycho-medical paradigm has grown up – particularly in recent years – an alternative way of understanding special needs. This paradigm – the 'interactive' or 'organizational' (Clark *et al.* 1995a) paradigm – acknowledges differences between individual children as both real and significant. However, it does not view these differences *alone* as adequately accounting for the failure of children within mainstream schools. Rather, it is the failure of those schools to respond with sufficient insight and flexibility to children's characteristics that results in educational failure. Since this paradigm sets particularly high store by the values of social integration, non-segregation and participation in a common curriculum seen as an entitlement for all children, it follows that the appropriate response to educational failure is to interrogate and reform the characteristics of schools rather than the characteristics of children (Ainscow 1994; Dyson 1990b; Skrtic 1991a).

These paradigms are not 'merely theoretical'. On the contrary, each has its distinctive implications for practice at three levels, if not more: school organization, teacher expertise, and underpinning values. To take each of these in turn:

- *School organization* The psycho-medical paradigm, on the one hand, requires forms of school organization in which remedial and adapted-curriculum-type activities can take place. That is, it requires settings that are more or less segregated, ranging from separate special schools at one end of the continuum to apparently 'integrated' classrooms at the other end, in which, none the less, pupils are effectively placed on separate tracks and offered altern-ative curricula (Hart 1992; Thompson and Barton 1992). The interactive paradigm, on the other hand, requires restructured mainstream schools in which separate forms of provision give way to a more flexible and responsive approach in regular classrooms.
- *Teacher expertise* The psycho-medical paradigm calls for special educators with a clearly-defined expertise which is different from that offered by mainstream educators. This expertise will allow them to address directly and effectively those aspects of their pupils' learning which make them 'special'. The interactive para-digm tackles the same issue by calling not for specialist expertise, but for an extended and enhanced form of 'general' teaching expertise, placing emphasis on the need for regular teachers to develop their skills to the point where they can routinely respond to a wide range of individual differences (Ainscow 1994).
- *Underpinning values* Working from assumptions about the de-ficits and disabilities which children with special needs 'suffer', the psycho-medical paradigm places particularly high value on actions which, where possible, cure or ameliorate those deficits and, at least, protect and care for their vulnerable victims. The special school, therefore, is seen as a caring environment; the adapted curriculum is seen as a means of protecting children from un-manageable demands; and the remedial group is seen as a curative intervention which takes precedence over whatever is going on in the mainstream classroom. The interactive paradigm, on the other hand, allocates the highest value to notions of participation, access and equality. It sees special forms of provision as forms of institutionalized discrimination and 'remediation' as a subtle and pernicious means of exclusion. For this paradigm, participation in

the social world of the regular classroom is more important than (and not incompatible with) protection, and access to a common curriculum is an entitlement that takes precedence over illusory forms of remediation and cure (Ballard 1995).

It is not difficult to see the connection between the paradigms we have thus characterized and the two national approaches to integration identified by Lise Vislie. The attempt to integrate by reforming and extending special education into mainstream schools would appear to be based on the psycho-medical paradigm with its assumptions about the necessity of special provision, even in a mainstream setting. The view of integration as essentially about the reform of mainstream schools is equally clearly informed by the interactive paradigm, with its assumptions about enhanced and flexible mainstream classrooms as the starting-point for meaningful responses to individual differences.

This, it seems to us, offers two explanations for Vislie's finding that special-education-focused integration is relatively ineffective. First, as Vislie herself points out, a move towards integration which is premised on the psycho-medical paradigm is self-contradictory, for it is precisely that paradigm which made segregation seem legitimate and rational in the first place. The attempt to persuade mainstream schools to accept responsibility for educating children with special needs whilst at the same time reaffirming the specialness and difference of those children, and emphasizing the specialist expertise necessary for their effective education, is doomed to failure (Dyson 1990a, 1991). At best, it will lead mainstream schools to replicate specialist forms of provision and to demand increasing levels of resources to support this provision. At worst, it will lead schools to outright rejection of problematic children.

Second, the psycho-medical paradigm, by focusing on the specialness of children and the special provision to be made for them, offers no rationale or mechanism for intervention in the workings of regular schools and classrooms. And yet, as advocates of the interactive paradigm point out, it is those very workings which play a significant part in determining which children succeed and remain 'ordinary', and which children fail and become 'special'. Once again, there are best and worst case outcomes from this position. At best, the education system commits itself to resource-intensive and ultimately inefficient forms of support for individual children in mainstream schools, when some reform of those schools might be less costly and more effective (the case of 'in-class support teaching' in the United Kingdom is an example of this (Allan *et al.* 1991; Hart 1986)). At worst, children with special needs are 'integrated' into an environment which has failure built in. We would argue strongly, therefore, that integration, if it is to be both manageable and effective, is about much more than the relocation of children from special to mainstream provision. Indeed, it is about much more than the replication of special provision in mainstream settings. Rather, it is about a paradigm shift which has implications for the way schools are organized, the way teachers teach, and for the values which underpin the whole education system. In particular, this paradigm shift requires a refocusing, away from the specialness of children and the special forms of provision they are seen to 'need', and towards the nature of mainstream schools and regular teachers and their ability to respond to a wide range of individual differences amongst their pupils.

Such a shift would be a major undertaking if it were restricted to policy-makers at national level. However, we know that special needs is something which is not constructed simply at the level of policy and the structuring of national systems. On the contrary, policy and systemic structuring simply set the context for the construction of special needs at the level of individual teachers and individual schools (Slee 1995; Ware 1995). We know that educational reforms which fail to engage with such constructions are doomed to failure (Fullan 1991a). And, finally, we are beginning to see how these local constructions emerge from peculiarly local factors, as well as from the broader national context (Clark *et al.* 1995a).

This knowledge, we believe, puts us in a position to redefine the project of 'integration' in a way which would have been difficult if not impossible when countries such as the United States and the United Kingdom began to move down this road two decades and more ago. That project is a complex and daunting one which cannot be accomplished simply through a process of centralized reform. None the less, there are specific steps that can be taken, and it is to these that we now wish to turn.

REFORMING MAINSTREAM SCHOOLS

Special responses in mainstream schools

There is a sense in which the separation of special and mainstream education systems in any country can be seen as self-perpetuating.

In so far as a special school sector exists, mainstream schools are likely to be offered 'perverse incentives' to narrow the range of students for which they cater and to avoid developing effective forms of special educational provision. The ready availability of special school placements effectively invites teachers and schools to subscribe to the psycho-medical paradigm, attributing those difficulties to within-child factors rather than to shortcomings in teaching and school organization.

If this situation is to be changed, there are, we believe, certain features which mainstream schools have to be helped to develop. Meaningful integration requires mainstream schools to develop their own 'special response systems' (Dyson 1993); that is, to have means of responding to the particular learning characteristics of students with special needs. In doing so, they have to achieve a difficult and delicate balance between treating all students as though they are identical on the one hand, and replicating special education systems within mainstream schools on the other.

Our recent work in British schools illustrates this point (Clark *et al.* 1995b; Dyson 1992). We identified what appeared to be quite contradictory developments in primary (elementary) and secondary schools. Primary schools tend to be small, to have little or no in-house special needs provision, and to depend heavily on the special services provided by the local education authority (LEA). In such schools, we detected a clear move towards the articulation of a school-level response to special needs, the development of a range of explicit teaching and support strategies, and the establishment of systems and procedures for assessing children's needs and taking co-ordinated action in respect of those needs.

Secondary schools, on the other hand, tend to be large enough to have their own in-house specialists, who have traditionally operated as internal providers of special education services. Here we detected a move *away* from such separate systems, an emphasis on responding to students' needs within regular classrooms and by means of the class teacher's expertise, and an attempt to blur the boundaries between special needs issues and wider issues of teaching and learning.

Our interpretation of these apparently contradictory developments is that, in order to respond to special needs without setting up forms of internal segregation, mainstream schools need sets of strategies and systems that are explicit and targeted on the one hand, but that are embedded within normal processes of teaching and hence within regular classrooms on the other hand. Such systems depend heavily on the skills and resources of regular classroom teachers. It is essential, therefore, both that these skills are enhanced through programmes of training and that the special responses that are established draw upon the skills and resources that class teachers already have (Ainscow and Tweddle 1989). 'Special teaching' thus becomes an extension of existing 'mainstream teaching' techniques – an enhanced use of group work, individualized materials, teacher exposition, problem-solving activities, and all the other strategies that teachers draw upon in their daily work. The mystique of the expertise of the special educator, which is reinforced by the existence of an extensive special school sector, is one that has to be dispelled if the integration process is to be meaningful.

However, it was evident in the schools we studied that class teachers were not left to work in isolation. The individual teacher and individual classroom were set in a context which provided them and their students with a flexible range of support. In broad terms, this support came in four forms:

- *Policies* Co-ordinated whole-school approaches to issues such as assessment, behaviour management, the use of information technology, parental involvement and so on.
- *People* Access to additional human resources such as special educators, parents and other adults working in the classroom, and external specialists (such as educational psychologists).
- *Places* Alternative places where learning could take place, such as resource centres, libraries, drop-in centres and facilities provided by other schools.
- *Programmes* Teaching programmes over and above those that class teachers could provide, such as one-to-one tuition, reading blitzes, curriculum extension and enrichment courses, special courses, and so on.

The existence of these key factors – appropriate and enhanced classroom teaching strategies, and flexible systems of support at the school level – appeared to have two effects. First, schools could respond to a range of special needs from within their own resources, without recourse to the special education system (Moore 1993a, 1993b). Second, they could respond to those needs largely within the context of their normal teaching procedures and hence within the common curriculum. These two effects amount to what we have called 'meaningful integration' as opposed to the replication of special education in mainstream schools.

Inclusive perspectives on teaching and learning

We found in our investigation that these responses to special needs both rested upon and contributed to particular perspectives on teaching and learning. A response to special needs by way of enhanced mainstream teaching was tending towards the redundancy of the psycho-medical model of special need. Rather than focusing on an ever more precise diagnosis of students' problems, or the formulation of ever more sophisticated remedial treatments, schools were seeking ways to enhance 'mainstream' teaching strategies to the point where they enabled students with special needs to learn within the common curriculum. To this extent, the task of 'special education' was becoming identical with the task of 'mainstream education'; both were seen as being about enabling individuals with distinctive characteristics to learn effectively.

This apparently abstract point has some very practical implications. In many schools – particularly secondary schools – special educators and special needs resources were increasingly being deployed in support of the learning of the full range of students. The focus for development was less on doing something 'special' for a minority of students than on enhancing the quality of provision for all, in the expectation that this would *ipso facto* constitute a response to special needs. Most schools we studied, for instance, had access to some level of in-class support teaching. Traditionally, this support has focused on one or two students with special needs in each class, who have been provided with extra help. However, many schools were using this support with the class as a whole, regardless of their level of 'special need', arguing that a higher level of adult attention was good for all students. A few schools had taken this argument even further, dismantling their special needs systems entirely and replacing them with systems (often led by a co-ordinator) for managing teaching and learning for all. Again, the argument was that responding to 'special' needs was simply a sub-set of responding to all needs.

These systems and structures in turn implied a particular view of the curriculum and of how learning should take place within the curriculum. As many within the inclusive education movement in the United States have pointed out (Fuchs and Fuchs 1994; Ware 1995), a traditional view of the curriculum as hierarchically organized knowledge and a traditional view of learning as the cumulative mastery of that knowledge are inherently inimical to the inclusion of those who cannot master the curriculum as quickly or completely as their peers. Inclusion – what we are calling meaningful integration – demands a more constructivist view, in which learners are seen as collaboratively building their own understandings rather than following predetermined paths of rote learning. Certainly, we identified a number of schools in which such views were beginning to emerge (Dyson *et al.* 1994), and in which the reconceptualization of the curriculum was becoming an essential constituent of meaningful integration. This has implications for the control of the curriculum at the national level, and is an issue to which we shall return in considering the policy context.

The school as problem-solving organization

There is a growing body of evidence and argument which suggests that the way schools are organized is not determined by the needs of their students, but rather that the needs of students emerge from the organization of the school (Ainscow 1993; Gartner and Lipsky 1987; Skrtic 1991a). In particular, the isolation of teachers in their classrooms, the sub-division of teaching expertise amongst subject or age-group specialists and the existence of separate special education systems internal and external to the school make it very difficult for teachers to respond effectively to the complex problems posed by students with special needs. A different sort of school, it is argued, based around problem-solving teamwork, is necessary for meaningful integration to take place.

In many of the schools we studied, there was evidence that collaborative problem-solving strategies were beginning to emerge. Teachers in these schools tended to support each other, sharing their expertise in order to develop special responses. This phenomenon was not simply a matter of the schools having a 'collaborative culture'. Rather, there were specific structures and systems which facilitated co-operative working. These included:

- in-class support teaching in which special educators and class teachers worked closely together on practical classroom problems;
- forms of professional consultancy in which special educators and class teachers were able to discuss particular problems and issues;
- problem-solving groups in which teachers pooled their expertise to assist one another in managing difficult situations;
- participatory decision-making structures which allowed teachers to plan together and to become involved in policy decisions.

Beyond this, some schools were developing means whereby the incidental learning which occurs as teachers collaborate together in problem-solving activities could be formalized. In particular, the focus on the quality of provision in mainstream classrooms as the key to special responses places a premium on schools being able to assess that quality and differentiate between effective and less effective practice. In some schools, therefore, special educators and/or teaching and learning co-ordinators were being asked to establish formal systems of quality assurance, monitoring and review. Typically, these systems made use of classroom observation, reviews of teaching materials and schemes of work, and feedback from students. These data were then used as the basis of a debate amongst the teachers concerned which in turn resulted in some commitment to action and development.

THE POLICY CONTEXT

Central–local relations: innovation through policy or practice?

In the previous section we have attempted to characterize the features of mainstream schools which were making them more able to promote 'meaningful integration'. We offer this characterization as a model which may be of use in determining the direction of school development in education systems which are engaged in integration initiatives. However, we are under no illusions either about the impact on schools of the local and national policy contexts within which they are located, or about the complexities of formulating such policy in a way which fosters the sorts of developments we are advocating. Accordingly, it is the policy context upon which we now wish to focus our attention.

   All policy-makers face a dilemma in their attempts to manage a process of educational reform in respect of special needs provision. On the one hand, issues such as the nature and extent of the special school sector, the placement of students with special needs, and therefore the move towards integration are matters of central concern, determined, as Vislie (1995) points out, by central legislation. On the other hand, all education systems, however centralized, have to cope with the enormous diversity of individual schools and the scope there is for misunderstanding, subversion, resistance and non-compliance with central initiatives (Fullan 1991a). This problem is, we would suggest, compounded in the field of special needs by the degree to which the values, beliefs and presuppositions of teachers and administrators – the 'paradigms' upon which they operate – are deeply implicated in both policy and practice (Clark *et al.* 1995a; Slee 1995; Ware 1995). It is, therefore, essential to understand the relationship between government policy on the one hand and school practice on the other and, in particular, to understand what sort of policy is most likely to promote meaningful integration.

Our first observation would be that the inability of central policy-makers to determine in fine detail practice at school level is not necessarily a disadvantage. The British schools which we have described are operating in a policy context which has given them, in some important respects, significantly increased levels of autonomy in recent years. Certainly, until very recently, there was no attempt at central government level to prescribe to schools what their approach to special needs should be, and some of the schools we studied were fiercely defensive of their ability to steer a course independently of the control and persuasion of local government. As a result, the approaches they developed were in many respects in advance of any guidance that was available at either local or national level. The role of teaching and learning co-ordinator, for instance, is not one that has been proposed in such guidance, but rather has emerged as a result of individual schools' own creative responses to their particular situations.

Schools were not operating in a policy vacuum, however, and we would wish in particular to highlight two areas where policy appears to have a significant impact. The first is in the way school-level innovations are responded to by policy-makers. We have found evidence in the British context (Clark *et al.* 1990; Dyson 1994) that there is an important role for local government in particular to play in supporting school developments. The initiatives which emerge from schools are in need of encouragement, support and guidance in the first instance, but also subsequently of evaluation and dissemination – at least if they are to be more than temporary blooms. We found, for instance, that some of the earliest and most enduring integration initiatives in the United Kingdom were not determined by central government at all, and were only lightly managed by local government. Essentially, they were school initiatives, which were supported and nurtured by their LEAs, but which only subsequently became part of LEA policy and, indeed, never entirely became part of national policy. The notion of 'mapping backwards to policy'

(Elmore 1989), of formulating policy on the basis of emerging practice rather than vice versa, is one which has considerable attraction in a field where change is so dependent on shifts in paradigm at the individual and school levels.

The second form of policy impact suggests a more proactive role for central government. Most of our work has been undertaken in the period following the introduction of a National Curriculum in England and Wales. For the first time, what should be taught in schools was set out in some detail as an entitlement and a right for all children. Moreover, the regulations governing the curriculum were accompanied by guidance (National Curriculum Council 1989a, 1989b) which forcefully articulated the principled view that students with special needs shared in this entitlement, and that the immediate task of schools was to ensure that such students had as full access to the common curriculum as was possible. This position has subsequently been reinforced by mechanisms for the inspection of schools, and for ensuring their accountability for special needs provision (Department for Education 1994; OFSTED 1992).

We have argued elsewhere (Dyson *et al.* 1994) that, in some cases at least, this articulation of principle supported by specific requirements led schools to rethink their special responses in ways which led to more meaningful forms of integration. We would, therefore, support arguments that there is a role for a 'moral authority' (Housden 1993) which stands above individual schools, and whose role it is to articulate value positions on behalf of the community as a whole and ensure that those values are realized in practice (Corbett 1994; Dyson 1994; Housden 1993; Moore 1993a, 1993b). In particular, we share the doubts of many of these writers about the inclination of autonomous schools to make themselves responsive to the needs of problematic students, and who argue for an advocacy role beyond the school on behalf of such students.

The implications of these observations for policy are, we believe, well captured in Hargreaves' (1994) recent commentary on school restructuring programmes in Canada and the United States. He argues that there are fundamental dilemmas facing such programmes in terms of the attractiveness to policy-makers of top-down restructuring versus the counter-claims of bottom-up, school- and teacher-led development. He argues that the emphasis must be on the latter, but not to the extent that overarching values are sacrificed. As he puts it:

in relaxing and relinquishing administrative control, the challenge of restructuring in postmodern times is also one of not losing a sense of common purpose and commitment with it. In trading bureaucratic control for professional empowerment, it is important we do not trade community for chaos as well.

(Hargreaves 1994: 63)

This is precisely the challenge we see facing many education systems as they move towards fuller and more meaningful integration. The solution we advocate is a central policy which is formulated with the intention of articulating community values, providing advocacy for the vulnerable, and imposing essential obligations and standards – but which respects the diversity of the education system, supports local innovation, and stops short of prescribing the fine detail of practice.

With this in mind, we wish to suggest some specific areas to which education systems might pay particular attention.

The centrality of school managers

It is evident that managers of education at the local level – the headteachers and the authorities to whom they are accountable – have a measure of autonomy in most education systems. The consequence is that heads become 'key determiners of reality' (Sharp and Green 1976). The way that educational issues are understood and responded to within schools is heavily determined by their attitudes, beliefs and values. In consequence, it is our consistent finding that the response made by a particular school to special needs is intimately bound up with the head's view of special needs. In particular, the common integration strategy of introducing special educators into mainstream schools as advocates for students with special needs is not, without the head's full and active support, sufficient to bring about the necessary developments in the school's practice and approach to special needs.

The implication, it seems to us, is twofold. First, any efforts at development, training, persuasion or compulsion must be addressed to the head and other key local managers. It is the constant complaint of special educators in the United Kingdom that training is directed at them when it is their headteachers who should be hearing the messages. Second, any advocacy of integration must accord with the concerns and priorities of headteachers and managers. Since, by definition, their prime concerns must be with the learning of the majority of their students, any advocacy of integration as something which benefits the minority at the (possible) expense of the majority is unlikely to succeed. It is for this reason, among others, that we have presented a model of integration which sees it as part of a wider concern for the teaching and learning of all students.

It is also, we would suggest, essential that school managers, in addition to this advocacy, be made accountable for provision for students with special needs at least as fully as they are for all other students. The English and Welsh education systems have recently suffered some minor traumas as some schools have used their new-found autonomy to avoid responsibility for such students. Integration necessarily means surrendering some measure of control over provision for students with special needs to the headteachers of mainstream schools. All national systems, therefore, need to consider mechanisms for making headteachers accountable for their schools' responses to special needs. In the United Kingdom, this has meant both the establishment of formal accountability procedures (referred to above) and the careful consideration of how the delegation of resources to schools can create incentives and disincentives which operate as a mechanism of control (Lunt and Evans 1993).

The role of clusters

Given our mistrust both of top-down reform and of entirely autonomous schools, it is with interest that we note the emergence of clustering in the British context (Dyson and Gains 1993; Gains 1994; Lunt *et al.* 1994). Such clusters are groups of schools which collaborate more or less closely in developing their responses to special needs. They thus generate various economies of scale, but more importantly, there is some evidence that they achieve a certain broadening of perspectives within participating schools which gives them a greater sense of responding to the needs of a community rather than to their own self-interest (Dyson 1994). The development of these clusters will need to be followed closely. In the meantime, their promotion may offer a way forward, particularly for education systems which lack an 'intermediary body' (Cordingley and Kogan 1993) able to offer the sort of leadership which English and Welsh LEAs can still (more or less) manage.

The curriculum

In most education systems, central government is able to exercise a greater or lesser degree of control over what is taught in schools. We have already alluded to the role played by the National Curriculum in developments in the United Kingdom, and to the association between meaningful integration and constructivist views of curriculum and learning. These need to be linked, for where meaningful integration is the aim, two characteristics of the curriculum are crucial:

• that the curriculum be formulated in such a way that meaningful participation is possible by all students, regardless of their individual characteristics;
• that such participation should be a right for all children.

The British experience suggests strongly that the declaration of curriculum participation as a right may actually be counter-productive from the point of view of integration if that curriculum is not one in which all students actually can participate. The linking of these two characteristics, therefore, is a difficult but essential strategy for education systems aiming to promote meaningful integration.

CONCLUSION

The dilemma for anyone writing about how integration might be promoted is that strategies which are effective in one national context might be quite inappropriate for another. It is not simply the nature of the integration process itself which differs from country to country, but systems of school management, the extent of central control, the characteristics of curriculum, the conceptualization of special needs and, indeed, understandings of the purposes of education itself. As Booth (1995) points out, there are real dangers in believing that we all speak a common language in this field.

The general principles we have tried to identify in this chapter, therefore, are no more than that. They are not so much a blueprint for action as a heuristic which educators and policy-makers seeking to promote integration in a wide variety of contexts can use to interrogate and illuminate their own situations. We wish to conclude, therefore, by summarizing these principles:

• Meaningful integration is essentially a process of transforming mainstream schools rather than reforming special education.

- It is a process of 'transformation' because it depends crucially upon paradigmatic shifts on the part of educators and policy-makers in the mainstream system.
- It depends upon assimilating questions of special needs provision into questions about teaching and learning for all students.
- This in turn demands particular forms of 'special response' in schools, and particular understandings of learning and curriculum.
- Such transformations cannot be legislated into being; they have to emerge from local innovation.
- However, local innovation can be supported, catalysed and guided by central advocacy and by mechanisms of both support and accountability.

We suggest that it is the adoption of principles such as these, rather than the process of legislative reform alone, which will lead in the future not only to more integration, but to more meaningful integration.

Chapter 6

Critical elements for inclusive schools

Gordon L. Porter

INTRODUCTION

The debate and discussion concerning the education of students with disabilities is very much alive among educators in Canada. Traditional methods and service systems are under increasing pressure to accommodate demands for more equality, more equity and more inclusion. The Canadian legal and policy framework increasingly encourages, and in many cases requires, the instruction of students with special needs in regular education classrooms alongside their non-disabled peers (*Bill 85* 1986; Porter and Richler 1990).

This chapter outlines how the organization of schooling can help ensure the achievement of equity for students with disabilities through inclusion. The development of inclusionary education programmes in Canada during the last decade provides the context for the discussion. Three principal factors are identified as critical to achieving inclusionary schools and classrooms. First, effective leadership in policy, administration, and programme implementation is discussed. Second, the establishment of a new role for the school-based special educator is described. Third, strategies that provide support for the classroom teacher teaching in an inclusive classroom, including staff development strategies, peer problem-solving teams, inclusive curriculum and instruction strategies, as well as 'multilevel instruction', are outlined. The creation of inclusive educational programmes for students with disabilities is linked to the creation of quality schooling for all students.

CONTEXT

In Canada (and the United States) the organization of schooling is shaped by the province or state, where legislation and goals are developed and the framework for policy, organizational structure and financing of education is established. This mandate is passed to a 'district', meaning a workable cluster of schools with some threads of mutual interest, most often based on sense of community or geographic area. The Canadian province of New Brunswick, which will be the main focus for this chapter, has school districts organized on the basis of both geography and language. There are eighteen school districts – twelve English and six French – ranging in size from 3,000 to 15,000 students.

The experience of one of the English language school districts, School District 12, will provide the context for most of the factors noted in this chapter. School District 12 has fourteen schools and approximately 5,000 students spread over an area of 7,200 square kilometres. In the small towns and villages of the district, it is usually quite clear what the 'community' or 'neighbourhood' school for each student should be. Some urban school districts in Canada serve 90,000 to 100,000 students, and the neighbourhood school is not quite as easily identifiable.

Full inclusion of all students is the starting-point for educational programming according to the legislation and policy of the province as well as the school district (*Bill 85* 1986; School District 12 1985). The thrust of this policy is that all children, including those with the most severe disabilities, should enter school with an assured right to placement in the regular classroom. Other alternatives may be necessary from time to time, but only when every effort has been made to make the regular classroom situation feasible, and only when alternatives are clearly in the student's best interests. As a result, students with special needs or disabilities attend the school they would attend if they were not disabled and are placed in a regular class with their age peers.

Some of the components necessary to make this policy a practical reality for children will now be described. After an examination of issues relevant to the provincial (or state) level, the issues most related to the district and school levels will be reviewed.

LEADERSHIP FACTORS

Philosophy

First, an inclusive approach requires an educational philosophy that is committed to the improvement of instructional strategies, school programmes and the most effective and equitable use of available resources. Educational improvement is not seen in terms of 'defective students' (Skrtic 1991b), and how their defects or disabilities might be cured, but in terms of how educators can improve programmes and practices to meet student needs.

Funding

All educational funding in New Brunswick comes directly from the provincial government and there is no local taxation for educational purposes. This approach was implemented twenty-five years ago to achieve fiscal equity throughout the province. The Ministry of Education funds 'special education' or 'student services' by providing a per-pupil grant based on the total student population of the district. For example, with 5,000 students and a grant of $325 per student, District 12 would have $1.625 million to spend on special services.

The use of this block-funding approach to fund special needs support services has several advantages. First, it eliminates the need to justify funding based on the disability of individual students. The result is less focus on disability and greater focus on support services to teachers and all students with special needs. Second, this approach does not encourage or reward the district for designating students as 'defective' or disabled. This approach assumes that every classroom, every school, and thus every district, will need a certain level of support services, simply because the educational system serves a heterogeneous population of students.

District leadership

An additional benefit of the funding approach described above is that it stimulates responsibility and accountability within both the school and the district. Additional funds cannot be obtained from the central authorities and local taxes cannot be raised to pay for more programmes or services. Responsible administrators are thus accountable for the effective allocation of resources, and must constantly seek better ways of meeting needs within the available funding. Creating an inclusive school system requires visionary leadership in overall programme and policy. Administrative leadership is also required to develop new programmes and practices as well as their effective implementation. With this leadership in place, a school district can establish the basis for an organizational culture based on collaboration and problem-solving that will facilitate the creation of inclusive schools. Administrators with general responsibilities, as well as those who work in the student services area, must articulate a clear and coherent vision for the educational programme of the district. This must be communicated to members of the staff, parents, students and the community. Developing a statement of beliefs for the education of exceptional students that is shared by those in leadership positions is an essential step in developing cohesion in programme and policy. The development of policies and programmes and their subsequent implementation will be more effectively accomplished if this exists.

A NEW APPROACH TO SPECIAL EDUCATION

In many parts of Canada (and the United States) the expansion of special education has resulted in the creation of parallel systems for the administration and delivery of regular and special education services (Skrtic 1991a). Many jurisdictions, with the most 'mature' and 'comprehensive', or traditional, special education services, have evolved to the point where the regular and special education systems exist separately and relate to each other only in the most theoretical way. The development of a parallel special education system has been harmful, not only because it excludes exceptional students and prevents their contact with non-disabled peers, but also because of the effect it has on the regular education system. A school system that hands over all students with learning problems and disabilities to a separate education structure undermines its ability to be a holistic unit that serves all students (Porter 1986).

The pervasive development of dual systems has led to repeated calls for reform to resolve the negative effects of this organizational 'disjointedness' (Gartner and Lipsky 1987; Reynolds *et al.* 1987; Stainback and Stainback 1984; Will 1986). In District 12, this 'disjointedness' has not occurred because of the rural nature of the area and the relatively late development of what have come to be the common elements of a fully developed special education system. This 'primitive' level of development has been identified as a critical factor in a number of jurisdictions where inclusion or integration of students with disabilities has been successful (Porter and Richler 1990). In many of these jurisdictions what was known as 'Special Education' is now called 'Student Services', and

Table 6.1 Alternative perspectives on special education practice

Traditional approach	Inclusionary approach
Focus on student	Focus on classroom
Assessment of student by specialist	Examine teaching/learning factors
Diagnostic/prescriptive outcomes	Collaborative problem-solving
Student programme	Strategies for teacher(s)
Placement in appropriate programme	Adaptive and supportive regular classroom environment

the change is more than in name. Table 6.1 sets our the difference in perspective that exists between the traditional special education view and the inclusive view.

As table 6.1 indicates, the focus of the 'inclusionary approach' is to support the regular school programme, that is the classroom teacher, the school principal and others, in achieving the goal of inclusive education. This approach recognizes that learning problems are contextual. They exist within the context of a particular environment, a specific classroom with a specific teacher and specific students. The curriculum, lesson design and instructional strategies employed by the teacher all influence the degree to which exceptional students can be well served in that classroom. A commitment to integrated or inclusionary education means teachers, schools and the community oblige themselves to resolve problems that arise in classrooms and schools in a way that respects the right of each student to be served as well as possible, and does not put the participation of the student with a disability at risk.

Traditional approaches to special education encourage the classroom teacher to refer instructional difficulties to experts who diagnose, prescribe and, invariably, provide alternative services for the student (Little 1985). The message inherent in this approach is that regular teachers are not qualified or competent to provide education to a student with a significant learning problem.

What is fundamental to an inclusionary approach in educating exceptional students is that the principal and the school staff accept responsibility for the progress of all students (Perner 1991). It follows that the classroom teacher must accept responsibility for the educational progress of all students in the class. Research is clear that teachers' attitudes and expectations have a significant impact on a student's self-concept and success (Purkey 1984).

An inclusionary programme requires a collaborative and consultation-based service delivery approach to replace the traditional 'student assessment-prescription-specialized instruction model'. The classroom teacher must believe that exceptional students belong and have confidence that they will learn.

Administrative leadership: practices and strategies

The administrative and co-ordinating functions that a 'district' can bring to the allocation of resources to a 'cluster' of schools is a distinct advantage for several reasons. First, it encourages district accountability and leadership in the educational enterprise. District leaders are experienced administrators who can articulate the philosophy and policy goals of the programme and help solve problems. Programme leadership is one of the essential factors in achieving an inclusive educational programme.

A district administrative structure also allows some adjustment to the resource allocation for individual schools. While per-student grants may meet the needs of 5,000 students taken as a whole, this approach may miss the mark when it is arbitrarily applied to schools ranging in size from 70 students to 600. This is particularly true when the situations change from year to year and students change schools three or four times during their school careers. Thus, the ability to provide additional supports in a specific school one year may be followed by the need to move some of the supports to another school the next year.

District-based team

An important component of the district organizational structure is the 'district-based student services team'. Competent district-based educators, acting as collaborative consultants, can provide constructive leadership and support for principals, teachers and other staff. They can provide additional support and facilitate access to additional resources as required. They also have an important role to play in programme monitoring and improvement. District-level consultants and specialists such as psychologists, speech/language pathologists and those knowledgeable in specific areas of disability are required in many situations. These personnel are often in short supply, and active recruitment and support for them are needed.

Regional service sharing

Many districts need to share specialized services with their neigh-bouring districts, due to factors such as size, low incidence of need and budget restrictions. This can be a very beneficial arrangement for a district, while also providing essential services to schools and students that might not be available otherwise. This is best illustrated by the provision of services to students with visual impairments, hearing impairments and severe learning/perceptual disabilities – all potentially low-incidence disabilities. Specialists provide consulta-tion to school districts based on their needs and itinerant teachers are allocated to districts depending on the need and available resources. A number of community agencies and services may act co-operatively with a school district in one role or another. Pre-school and early intervention programmes play an important part in pro-viding services to young children with disabilities. Districts can also co-operate with community agencies that provide vocational and job placement programmes. These agencies often can assist in planning and moving students from school to work. This form of co-operation and sharing of experience and expertise is invaluable.

A NEW ROLE FOR THE SPECIAL EDUCATOR

Most of the money spent on special education is allotted to teacher salaries. The redirection of financial resources, from direct service provision to students in segregated settings, to support for teachers working in heterogeneous classrooms, is one of the most critical factors in the creation of inclusive schools. In New Brunswick and School District 12, a significant role change was essential for school-based special education staff (Porter 1991). Special class teachers and resource teachers were reclassified as method and resource teachers (M&R teachers).

The M&R teacher's role was defined to emphasize collaboration and peer support to the regular class teacher. The M&R teacher is responsible for assisting the classroom teacher to develop strategies and activities to support the inclusion of exceptional students in the regular class. However, this model does not constitute team teaching, as some inclusionary models do, by having a special education teacher merge his/her students with those of a regular classroom teacher. This would not meet the requirement for 'natural distribu-tion' of students with disabilities since it places more such students in a single class than would occur in the absence of this strategy. It has the further effect of having the former 'special education teacher' provide support for only one regular class teacher.

The M&R teachers carry out a variety of activities, but all are designed to help teachers solve problems and work out the best alternatives for instruction. Among the M&R teacher's functions are the following:

- programme planning and development;
- programme implementation;
- assessment and prescriptive services;
- programme monitoring;
- communication and liaison;
- direct instruction.

It is essential that M&R teachers are not seen as experts, who should take responsibility for any difficulties of the regular teacher. Instead, they must be seen as someone who can assist the teacher in finding workable solutions to problems that occur in the class. One M&R teacher described the strategy this way:

> I had to make sure that the teacher had enough resources to work with. Also, if they were having any difficulty, I would see how I could assist them in making it easier for the child to participate in the classroom. I had to be in the classrooms at times monitoring what was going on and the way things were being handled, how the teacher and the student were adjusting and if there were any difficulties.

Experience, in most districts, indicates that method and resource teachers who have extensive classroom teaching experience, and who are regarded by their peers as competent classroom teachers, have the greatest success in this position (Porter 1991). In response to a survey, most of our M&R teachers stated that having regular class teaching experience was essential to their credibility with other teachers. One commented:

> I think experience as a regular class teacher is necessary. It would be a mistake to bring somebody totally new into the job. The good thing about having somebody who was a classroom teacher, especially from the same school or district, is that teachers see you as another teacher. I think that's good. You're more aware of what some of the problems are.

It is also necessary that the M&R teacher has specific knowledge relevant to the education of exceptional students. Post-graduate study in special education supplemented by regular in-service training while working in the area is preferred.

A school may be assigned one or more M&R teachers depending on the relative needs of the school and the funding available. There can be variation for specific reasons but schools generally receive one full-time position for each 8–12 regular classes in a school. Additional staff may be assigned to a school if an unusual number of students with significant needs are enrolled in a given school year or if the teaching staff is perceived to need more direct support. M&R teachers provide the professional support needed in planning, monitoring and evaluating, while teacher assistants provide physical support and various types of ongoing support in the classroom. In most cases, the need for more support can be satisfied by allocating additional paraprofessional time to the school staff. Adjustments to paraprofessional time can be made more easily and increasing this support is also more cost effective.

Since the M&R teacher works with students and parents, as well as teachers and administrators in highly varied circumstances, the need to be creative, flexible and responsive is evident. Although M&R teachers may set daily schedules for classroom work and other duties, they must be prepared to find time to handle an unexpected request for assistance from a teacher, or participate in a meeting called by the principal. Two M&R teachers describe this aspect of their work as follows:

> You have to find ways of being there. Teachers don't always like to arrange meetings, but they like to drop in. Maybe you're right in the middle of something, but you have to make yourself available for them when they're available.

> In the method and resource role you can plan a day, but very often you can only get into a couple of things that you wanted to do. So you have to be on your toes and be able to be versatile, to change your plans on the spot. In the classroom it's a much more organized day. You know exactly what's going to happen.

M&R teachers must be able to lead school staff in developing positive expectations for students with disabilities. They must have confidence in teachers, ensuring that teachers who previously have not taught students with special needs can and will respond positively to the challenge. They must have the persistence to keep digging for strategies to assist teachers and thus to help students. They must have a positive and optimistic outlook.

A unique demand on the M&R teacher is the regular and intensive teamwork required with classroom teachers, who may have limited experience of sharing responsibility and decision-making in their work. M&R teachers have identified organizational and communication skills, as well as the commitment to solve complex problems, as prerequisites for success in that role. Other skills needed include skill in facilitating meetings, diagnosing student needs, and establishing individualized educational programmes. M&R teachers must also acquire an extensive knowledge of curriculum structure, process and content.

Thus, a commitment to personal development and continuous learning becomes an important trait of M&R teachers. In some districts, M&R teachers have the equivalent of a full day of in-service training every month. This time may be used to deal with an issue of topical concern, to learn something new from a resource person or to share instructional or support strategies that are common to their work in district schools (Porter and Collicott 1992). The most significant outcome of this process is the development of a positive outlook toward challenges and an interest in creating and supporting change in school practices.

STRATEGIES FOR TEACHER SUPPORT

Staff development for classroom teachers

In New Brunswick, the classroom teacher is considered the primary resource in instructing exceptional students. This requires teachers to continually refine their skills or knowledge, as well as to develop new ones. Therefore, staff development at the school and district level is critical in order to develop successful integrated educational practices.

In District 12, an ongoing assessment of teachers' training needs is part of the district's commitment to inclusion. Priorities have included multilevel instruction, co-operative learning, providing enrichment through the curriculum, and dealing with students with behaviour problems. Personnel also identified collaborative problem-solving and the development of peer support groups as priorities.

Long-term support through staff development activities is critical in adapting traditional teaching practices to meet the educational needs of exceptional students. Staff development needs to be school-based and directed toward enhancing the teacher's problem-solving skills. Teachers must be intimately involved in the various steps of the process to improve their practices (Fullan 1991a). Collaboration with peers, M&R teachers and other classroom teachers must replace isolation and competition. The school environment must empower teachers by helping them to see themselves, and others, as effective problem-solvers. Barriers between staff members must disappear, leaving the level of trust necessary to gain new knowledge, skills and practices (Skrtic 1991a).

Problem-solving teams

Peer problem-solving teams provide a model of support that is based on the strengths of individual teachers. This process encourages classroom teachers to help their colleagues resolve instructional problems. Schools can use this procedure to secure efficient and effective help and, at the same time, keep the initiative for action in the hands of classroom teachers.

There are several variations of this model (Chalfont *et al.* 1979; Porter *et al.* 1991; Porter 1994), but the essence is a process designed to address a problem a teacher is having in a structured format, making effective use of time. When a teacher refers a problem to the group, team members generate possible alternatives. The teacher is able to select the options which seem most promising. One or more members of the team may provide follow-up support if needed. While the model may be varied to meet particular circumstances, it should include most of the following components:

- an effective and task-oriented chairperson;
- at least three volunteer teacher team members;
- teacher choice in selecting alternatives for implementation;
- agreement on follow-up and responsibility for monitoring;
- follow-up meeting to review progress;
- commitment of team to persist if required.

Peer problem-solving teams are a valuable tool that can reinforce the emphasis on school-based problem-solving and allow for direct, practical and positive assistance to teachers.

Inclusive curriculum and instructional strategies

An inclusionary approach to curriculum is required. This means a common curriculum for all students, which provides for multilevel instruction. Students at all levels are provided with opportunities for meaningful involvement in classroom activities. One M&R teacher observed that 'Most teachers feel much more at ease if we can take the regular programme and deal with that so these kids can still be a part of the class. They find it easier to cope that way'. This supports the development of a curriculum that is activity-based and allows students to learn from doing. An inclusionary curriculum provides both process and content that will facilitate students and teachers working together to achieve meaningful learning for every student.

Good teaching practices are appropriate to all students, as all students have learning strengths and individual learning styles. This applies to exceptional students as well as others. There is increasing evidence that exceptional students need little in the way of distinct instructional strategies. They may need more time, more practice or an individualized variation of approach, but not a strategy explicitly distinct from that used with other students.

Multilevel instruction

Multilevel instruction (Schulz and Turnbull 1984) is the name given to a major instructional initiative undertaken in District 12, enabling a teacher to prepare one main lesson with variations which are responsive to individual student needs (Collicott 1991). It is an alternative to preparing and teaching a number of different lessons within a single class. Multilevel instruction involves identifying the main concepts to be taught in a lesson; determining different methods of presentation to meet the different learning styles of students; determining a variety of ways in which students are allowed to express their understanding; and developing a means of evaluation that accommodates different ability levels.

The implementation of multilevel instruction has been a major focus of staff development activity in School District 12 since 1989. The main emphasis of the training plan for multilevel instruction has been to provide a staged introduction of the idea to the instructional staff of each school. Initially, individual school principals identified two or three teachers on staff who had demonstrated success with inclusion. Those teachers were typically well respected by other staff members and were willing to form a cadre to be trained and later train the rest of the school staff. M&R teachers, principals and vice-principals also received training in the fundamentals of multilevel instruction. Each school was subsequently required to develop a plan to provide all staff members with ongoing training in multilevel instruction. This was done through small-group training of classroom teachers followed by peer collaboration and coaching to develop and extend these newly acquired skills. Principals and vice-principals supported the implementation by monitoring the use of this instructional technique through teacher supervision and observations, and by creating opportunities for teachers to share successful strategies during staff meetings.

CONCLUSION

Michael Fullan, Dean of Education at the University of Toronto, an acknowledged expert on educational change, reform and improvement, has noted that reform in special education 'represents just about all the issues involved in bringing about educational reform'. Complexity and leadership are particularly difficult challenges. Fullan has noted that 'The solutions to inclusion are not easily achieved. It is complex both in the nature and degree of change required to identify and implement solutions that work. Given what change requires – persistence, co-ordination, follow-up, conflict resolution, and the like – leadership at all levels is required' (Fullan 1991b: ii).

In this chapter, the key factors in creating inclusive classrooms, leadership in policy and implementation, defining a new collaborative support role for the 'special education teacher', and supporting teachers in the transition to inclusion through selected school and classroom practices, have been examined. Organizational support for the actions discussed must be in place at the provincial (or state) level, the regional or school district level, and at the individual school level. These structures, programmes and policies must deliver the support needed by classroom teachers and their students. The commitment to equity, and thus inclusion, requires continuing efforts to build on these approaches. Doing so can permit schools to better serve students with disabilities while creating more effective schools for all students. One of the M&R teachers in School District 12 put it effectively as follows:

I think the biggest thing that we've done, other than integration, is to make teachers aware of the fact that all children are not learning at grade level, and that they have to teach them at their level and have them meet with success at that level. A lot of children are having their needs met, who before would have just been pushed along or ignored. Integration has caused teachers to address the whole situation differently.

Chapter 7

Integration developments in Member countries of the OECD

Don Labon

INTRODUCTION

The main frame of reference for this chapter is recent work undertaken by the Organization for Economic Co-operation and Development (OECD). Between 1990 and 1993 most of the then twenty-four Member countries of the OECD provided country reports on the education of children with special needs and produced accounts of a total of sixty-four studies of good practice relating to the teaching of these children in regular schools. All the countries concerned maintained integrationist policies with regard to children with special educational needs, and in about half of these countries fewer than 1 per cent of children were reported to be attending special schools. Practice, however, varied considerably from one country to another. Most of the material presented in this chapter is drawn from the two compilation reports arising from this project and published by the OECD (1995a).

The material is set out under the headings of eight issues emerging from the amalgamation of country reports and case studies as key issues relating to the success or otherwise of inclusive education programmes. They fall into three clusters: two issues concerning resources available within the regular schools; four issues concerning organization, both within individual schools and across groups of schools; and two issues that are largely external to the schools, though they can greatly influence what goes on in them.

RESOURCES ISSUES

Time

In supporting re-integration of children from special schools to regular schools, time allowances are often given to special school teachers: for example, to teach in the regular schools on a peripatetic basis once the children have been introduced there. But time allowances also need to precede children's introduction to the regular school, as there is much preparatory work to be done.

Consider an innovative programme designed to shift the focus of special education from special schools to regular schools, say at district or regional level within a country. The time commitments needed, from the stage at which the programme is first thought of to the stage at which it can be said to be completed, are considerable. The OECD compilation report based on material culled from the country reports ended with the presentation of a framework for a six-stage programme. These stages included the following.

1 *Identification* At this stage, provisional decisions are made as to which children may be integrated, and on what time-scale. For example, some children may move on a part-time basis from special classes to regular classes before others move from special schools to regular schools. Provisional decisions also need to be made as to feasibility and likely costs.

2 *Consultation* If the programme still looks desirable, feasible and affordable, prime candidates for early consultation include parents of disabled children, special education teachers, teachers in regular schools, and support staff in education, health and social work services.

3 *Assessment of existing strengths* As the success of an integration programme depends greatly on the attitudes and skills of class-room teachers in regular schools, some preliminary assessment needs to be made of the extent to which teachers likely to be affected already possess these attributes. Account also needs to be taken of the attitudes and skills of existing teachers in special schools, particularly if they are likely to shift into teaching or advisory work in regular schools, where they will need skills other than those they need in special schools.

4 *Target setting* This is the stage at which one moves from broad aims to specific objectives, each to be achieved within a planned time-scale. Targets need to be set for teachers, support staff and parents as well as for children, and the enterprise will need to be costed more precisely. Targets may include partial integration for some children and full integration for others.

5 *Implementation* 'Awareness raising' is likely to constitute a crucial early phase in implementation. The emphasis is usually on

reducing prejudices, allaying unrealistic anxieties and overcoming any preoccupation with disabilities rather than with learning potential. The people to be involved include a regular school's parents and teachers generally, and perhaps the children too, not just those concerned directly with special education. As some scepticism can continue even after programmes have had demonstrable success, awareness raising needs to be a continuing feature of integration programmes. In-service education and training (INSET) for teachers is essential, again on a continuing rather than a preliminary basis, with a particular focus on curriculum differentiation, along with the development of a continuum of support. As programmes are implemented in regular schools, their effects on special schools need to be taken into account and adjusted to.

6 *Evaluation* While this has been listed as the final stage, the monitoring of integration processes and evaluation of outcomes should in fact feature throughout integration programmes, not just at the end. Evaluation cannot be complete without counting the cost. This should be done over a fairly long time-scale, as integration programmes invariably require a relatively heavy input at their initial stages, and are likely to be less resource-intensive as they become established.

The value of providing time for re-integration should be considered in relation to the value of providing teaching time for 'preventative' work with children who start in regular schools but who, if they do not receive extra help, may become candidates for special schools. In developing preventative work, a staged plan similar to that already outlined needs to be worked out. When children with special needs are helped in integrated settings, time allowances should be enough to enable class teachers and special needs specialists not only to teach but also to plan, to confer, to measure and evaluate progress, and to undertake any INSET needed.

The amount of time needed for effective INSET can be appreciable, particularly when teachers are being helped to develop skills, not just to acquire knowledge. The following example, an extract from the OECD (1995a: 184) case study report, illustrates the point. Here the training materials designed for use by teachers in Australia took the form of an action research package. As part of the package, any teacher following it was able to draw on the expertise of a local support group of some three or four people, identified at the outset as being able to provide help and advice specifically relevant to the tasks envisaged.

In one trial, for example, the teacher had elected to work individually with a six year old boy with reading difficulties. Her support group consisted of a special education support teacher, a university lecturer and a special programmes coordinator. Following an initial planning meeting of the group, the teacher attended a workshop on action research run by the lecturer, then worked with the lecturer to plan a teaching programme. The programme involved extending the child's phonic ability, establishing a sight vocabulary and using this vocabulary in story writing.

The teacher was released from class duties sufficiently to undertake daily half hour or one hour sessions with the boy over a seven week period. As well as being given time to teach the child, the teacher allocated time to meet periodically with the members of the support group, for planning and monitoring purposes, and to write an evaluative report at the end of the programme. Gains, in addition to the boy's progress, included the teacher's increased skills, the interest of other school staff in undertaking similar work, and increased involvement of the parents, as voluntary classroom helpers, in the work of the school.

Skills

The example just given shows how a teacher can develop the skills needed to provide help through an individual teaching programme. However, class teachers must be able to help children with special needs not only individually but also as part of their work with the class as a whole. The following extract, drawn from the synthesis of the OECD (1995a: 56) country reports, provides a glimpse of what is involved.

Across OECD countries, teachers differentiating the curriculum are able to depart from teaching the whole class the same content at the same time. In doing so they set separate tasks for different groups within the class and occasionally, particularly where children have special needs, for individuals. Each group is likely to consist of children of similar levels of attainment, though it is possible to have a mixed ability group in which children contribute to a common task on the basis of their differing capabilities: for example, one may search for relevant information, another may summarise it, another may supply illustrations and so on. Whatever the grouping, the teacher can foster co-operative learning, whereby those children who can manage tasks help those who cannot.

Although tasks vary, all the children in the class are likely to be working to a common objective within the progression of the curriculum. For example, in a mathematics lesson concerned with handling data, a class of eight-year-olds might share the tasks of measuring the height of each member of the class and distributing the measures across five colour-coded categories: very short, short, medium etc. The majority, helped as necessary, would be able to graph the results. Those who could not, would probably be able to predict which children fell into which category and perhaps group the results using coloured blocks. The most able could be asked to work out the average and possibly construct pie charts.

As well as giving us an idea as to what differentiation means, this extract raises two important points. First, it makes it obvious that differentiation is a highly skilled activity. Second, it demonstrates the point that differentiation is not just a device for helping children with learning difficulties. It is a means of helping all the children in the class to progress as much as they can. In other words, it is good teaching.

There is a further point worth making here about teaching skills. The examples given so far are of teaching basic subjects; the first was of an individual literacy programme, the second was of a whole-class mathematics activity. When INSET in teaching methods appropriate to children with special needs is provided, it often focuses on literacy skills, perhaps with some consideration of numeracy. It is self-evident that this can be of value, particularly if it includes not only provision of relevant information but also monitored and assessed practical work for the teachers concerned.

Surely, though, in developing their skills, teachers need to be able to differentiate their teaching not just in basic subjects, but across the curriculum as a whole, and training should help them to do this. Science, for example, is also a subject in which class teachers may well need help if they are to match work to children's differing abilities, and it may be that some INSET sessions should aim at helping children develop their social skills. If teachers are not used to working together in the same classroom, they may need some training in team-teaching.

As teachers are the education industry's most expensive resource, and as the educational scene is continually changing, it can be argued that their training should continue periodically throughout their careers. This looks like a tall order, but of course much of a school's development of teachers' skills can be undertaken on a self-help basis, particularly if the school has someone with appropriate skills who has school-wide responsibilities for co-ordinating special needs work.

The following extract (OECD 1995a: 156), concerning one of the Swiss case studies, shows how INSET can be built into a school's working arrangements, occasionally drawing on expertise from outside. In this study, teaching staff in elementary schools operated in teams of four, each team consisting of three class teachers and one special needs specialist. Children with special needs were taught mostly in regular classes but were sometimes withdrawn for individual coaching. The timetable included an 'option branch' project, whereby classes were mixed up for fine arts and music activities.

Maintenance of this pattern required extensive cooperation within each team. Formal arrangements for consultation included weekly planning meetings among the four concerning the option branch project and weekly meetings among the three class teachers concerning particular subjects. In addition, the special needs specialist met each class teacher, fortnightly to discuss the children generally and at six month intervals to discuss and write reports on each of the children with learning disabilities. All the school staff attended weekly meetings concerning school matters generally.

Each class teacher and the special needs specialist met quarterly with the educational psychologist to plan support arrangements for children with special needs, and met periodically with parents. Other meetings with people from outside the school included six-monthly regional meetings of teachers engaged in integrated education.

ORGANIZATION ISSUES

Stages of provision

It was clear from the OECD case studies that there was still scope in many schools for further development towards the kind of continuum of special provision that enables children with special needs to be helped through various combinations of within-class support, withdrawal group work and individual tuition. The following extract (OECD 1995a: 156) shows how staff of one particular school were trying to develop such a continuum.

> The United Kingdom example is of an elementary school on the fringe of an industrial town with a relatively high level of unemployment. The school had a history of having provided, through special classes, for special needs across a geographical area beyond that of its own catchment.
>
> At the time of the OECD project visits in late 1991, there were 14 full-time teaching staff, 6.5 nursery nurses and two special support assistants. There were nearly 300 children on roll, of whom 46 had statements of special need. Many had physical disabilities as well as some learning difficulty, and a few had severe learning disabilities. Ten were fully integrated in regular classes and the remaining 36 were distributed across five special classes. Individual structured integration programmes operated in each special class. The school also ran a nursery, offering 46 part-time places, three of which were taken up by preschool children with statements.
>
> The head was successfully encouraging class teachers to take on children from the school's special classes, thus progressively implementing one of the school's main aims, as stated in the school handbook: 'Through the shared activities it is hoped that understanding of one another's strengths will occur as well as acceptance of one another's weaknesses.'
>
> An important aspect of school ethos was an emphasis on integration as a means of educating children, rather than as marking stages at which those with special needs had 'caught up' with the rest. A striking feature of the school was the very real acceptance among 'ordinary' children of those with special needs. Both within the classroom and outside it, children would spontaneously and unostentatiously give a helping hand to those needing it. The flexible integration arrangements necessitated complex and ever-changing timetables, and these were facilitated considerably by the fact that special and regular class arrangements were all actively managed by the head of the school.
>
> . . .pupils would go individually to the nursery with a nursery nurse

– it was felt that it was beneficial for them to see other, more advanced, children playing and thereby have the opportunity to copy them. Those with less severe difficulties would join a mainstream class for an hour's activities in the afternoon. Mornings were usually devoted to specific language and number work throughout the school and the special classes operated their own curriculum with individual programmes operated through individual and group work. At times, just one or two pupils would be in a mainstream class; at others, a whole special class would be out in mainstream with or without a nursery nurse. Some pupils joined another mainstream class and were taught by their teacher, while others would accompany their special class teacher while she went to a mainstream classroom and taught the class, freeing the regular class teacher to go elsewhere (for example, to teach a specialist subject). Some of the most severely handicapped pupils in the special unit would integrate with another special class.

The case studies undertaken for the OECD project included several examples of attempts to implement whole-school policies for meeting special educational needs in regular schools, and various problems in implementing such policies came to light. It was clear that the context within which the school was working could do much to help or hinder implementation. The composite case study report identified the following conditions as facilitating the implementation of a whole-school inclusion policy:

1 National legislation requiring, or at least promoting, integration.
2 Regional and district policies supporting integration.
3 Allocation of national and local special education resources in a manner conducive to integration.
4 Wholehearted promotion, monitoring and evaluation, by the school's senior management team, of the school's integration policy and its implementation.
5 Flexible organization of classes, permitting groupings of various kinds and some interchange of staff roles.
6 Learning programmes at various levels, for individual and for group work. Programmes to develop social as well as academic skills. Time to develop, evaluate and modify these programmes.
7 Staff with general credibility and with special needs expertise, able to offer in-class support and withdrawal teaching, and able to provide consultation and in-service training for class teachers.

8 Arrangements enabling all staff to consult, to co-operate, to plan, and to develop and maintain appropriate attitudes and skills.

Modifications to special schools

As countries pursue policies for inclusive education, the proportion of children with special needs being educated in special schools decreases, and this process carries various implications for INSET. For example, should time available for INSET focus on work with children with special needs in regular schools, and for what changes of role should teachers in special schools be prepared? Several of the case studies contributing to the OECD project referred to outreach work based on special schools as a means of enabling staff of special schools to contribute to INSET in regular schools. Success was not easy to achieve; the composite report identified the following as conditions conducive to success:

1 The children, parents and teachers concerned, teachers in the special school as well as those in the regular schools, are motivated towards integration.
2 Facilities exist to ensure that the special school teachers undertaking outreach work develop the assessment, training and advisory skills needed.
3 If those advising in regular schools are based in the special school, their work helps teachers to cope for themselves, rather than to rely on special teachers to look after the children presenting significant difficulties.
4 If those based at the special school undertake extensive advisory work in the regular schools, they have appropriate arrangements with local authority services, thus avoiding duplication of effort.
5 If those based at the special school rely on local authority based advisers to undertake all but the most specialized support work, rather than take it on themselves, staffing and expertise in the local authority services are sufficient for this to occur.
6 Outreach staff and staff in regular schools have sufficient flexibly allocated time to negotiate, plan, evaluate and develop their skills further as well as to teach.
7 Outreach staff negotiate specific and finite arrangements, including learning targets, for the support they are to provide.
8 Special school staff arranging integrated placements take due account of staffing levels in the regular schools as well as of the expertise and goodwill available.

9 Special school staff constructively take account of any effects their outreach work may have on the reputation within the community of the regular schools with which they are concerned.

10 Special school staff monitor both the progress of children for whom they undertake outreach work and the professional development of the teachers they help, using the results to evaluate and revise their provision.

11 Outreach staff develop and maintain a stock of appropriate support materials, ensuring that regular school teachers and children can have access to them when they need them.

12 Allocation of special school staff time and expertise to the school's various teaching, resourcing, advisory and training functions is such that all these functions remain viable.

13 Special school staff consider carefully the range of expertise they are to offer, attempting to tailor this to meet local needs.

Support systems

It was clear both from the OECD country reports and from the associated case studies that class teachers implementing inclusive education policies are likely to require continuing support, both from staff based within the school and from people based outside it. The development of systems of support invariably raises the question, equivalent to that concerning the guards in Juvenal's Rome ('Quis custodiet ipsos custodes?'), as to who should support the supporters. The following extract (OECD 1995a: 157) from the composite case study report demonstrates one way in which a continuum of provision for special needs in regular schools can be woven seamlessly into a system of support established at district level.

> The Canadian example comes from a New Brunswick district with a strong commitment to integration and a long history of integration practice, including closure of the district's two special schools in the early 1980s and, in accordance with explicit district policy, subsequent shifts from special to regular classes. All children, including those with special needs, then had right of access to education in their own local schools.
>
> By 1993 an important feature of the organization of each school in the district was the student services team, consisting

of the school head or deputy head, a guidance counsellor, a methods and resource teacher, and teaching assistants. The district's allocation of staffing to schools was largely on the basis of number of children on roll, but varied to some extent according to nature of catchment area. For example, one methods and resource teacher would be allocated to every 200 or so on roll. In the elementary and secondary schools visited as part of the OECD project, pupil–teacher ratios generally were between 12:1 and 16:1, with between 300 and 600 on roll. From the point of view of integration, a key role appeared to be that of the methods and resource teacher.

> The methods and resource teacher's primary duty is to assist classroom teachers in developing instructional programmes for exceptional students. Their role focuses on providing collaborative consultation, teacher to teacher support, and assistance with problem solving. Teacher assistants provide the one-to-one support needed for individual students with severe disabilities, and the overall classroom assistance teachers may require for less intensive situations. Guidance counsellors focus directly on personal student problems as opposed to instructional issues and are part of the student services team in the school. Cooperative education coordinators at the junior and senior high school level also serve on the student services team. They assist in arranging job placements for exceptional students. This is an essential part of the overall integration programme, although it is based on integration into the community.

Another important aspect of the methods and resource teachers' work was receipt of in-service training, on a bi-weekly basis, run by district support services based externally to the school. Topics included multilevel instruction, cooperative learning, problem solving and non-violent crisis intervention. Part of the methods and resource teacher's job was then to help other members of staff to acquire these skills too. All staff with integrated children in their classes were allocated 'school enhancement days', which enabled them to consult other adults, plan assignments, visit other schools and so on.

Incidentally, provision of support for class teachers engaged in inclusive education is not exclusively the province of professionals. In some OECD countries parental and community involvement featured strongly as part of the system of support available both to schools and to parents. The following extract (OECD 1995a: 164) from the case study report submitted by the United States is illuminating.

> The school organizes foster grandparent, parent volunteer, and peer tutoring programs which are available to all students. Students with moderate or severe disabilities have a big brother/sister program available on a limited basis, particularly for students labeled severely emotionally disturbed. Parent support groups offer some assistance to parents of students with moderate and severe disabilities.
>
> Some local business and community organizations have donated equipment for students with severe disabilities. Local religious and athletic organizations offer community recreation programs, especially for older students who need career or vocational experiences. The local mental health agency is involved with a few students with moderate and severe disabilities.
>
> Some businesses and business organizations provide opportunities for students with disabilities who are in financial need. In addition, other organizations often provide opportunities for students with moderate and severe disabilities to attend summer camps or local recreation camps, and will under certain conditions purchase or loan to families necessary equipment.

Co-operation across schools

Within a given region, regular schools developing integration policies may develop links with other regular schools similarly engaged. As such links become formalized, the networks thus created can be powerful aids to the dissemination of good practice. Extensive networking was reported in a Dutch case study (OECD 1995a: 158) of twenty-eight co-operating elementary schools, together aiming to maintain children with special needs within the regular school system. These arrangements fostered extensive co-operation among teachers, provided mutual support, facilitated exchange of ideas, and enabled teachers to develop the attitudes, confidence and skills required for the successful teaching of children with special needs.

The schools were relatively small, averaging about 100 on roll, each school had two teachers concerned particularly with special needs, and their cooperation was coordinated by the region's education advice centre. If a school was unable to provide effectively for a particular child, placement in another of the schools was negotiated through the advice centre, thus enabling the child to have the opportunity of a fresh start. With regard to their work generally, the staff of the schools operated a common policy, collaborated in working groups concerned with various aspects of curriculum development (at the time of the OECD project there were 16 such groups in operation), shared materials, agreed on teaching methods and attended in-service courses run at the education advice centre.

EXTERNAL ISSUES

Public opinion

The OECD country reports made it clear that in many countries the advocacy of parents of children with disabilities has for long been a driving force in the development of special education. With regard to the majority of children with special needs, this force has generally been in favour of integration, though this is not necessarily the case where children's disabilities are severe. The extent of parental involvement in special educational provision varies considerably, ranging from occasional token contact to full participation in classroom teaching and in school management. The case study compilation report, drawing on country reports, case studies and an enquiry specially commissioned for the project, presented the following summary of features of good practice in parental and community involvement:

1 At all stages of national developments in integration, representatives of parent organizations are involved on a consultative basis.
2 As district and within-school integration programmes are developed, parents of children with special needs, along with representatives of the communities more generally, are consulted from the outset of each stage and are invited to participate.
3 When parents of children with special educational needs seek to initiate or further develop integration programmes, their views are taken as seriously by decision-makers as are those of professionals.
4 Parents are treated as partners in assessment, decision-making and review when their children are being considered by staff of schools and external support services with a view to special educational provision.

5 Parents of children with special educational needs are represented on the governing bodies of schools.
6 Where appropriate, parents and other members of the community are encouraged to be present in classrooms and to share in the work of the schools.
7 Parents of children with special needs, particularly parents of preschool children, are helped by professionals to develop the skills needed to teach their own children.

Funding

If teachers are to be encouraged to help children with special needs in regular schools, appropriate training should be supported by funding mechanisms that take account of the extra resources required for their effective education. While such resources are greater than those needed for the majority of children, information collected by the OECD suggests that they are generally still below the levels commonly supporting special schooling. A further OECD study, currently being carried out, is designed to provide a more detailed comparison of costs of educating children with disabilities in special and regular schools.

One funding mechanism can be to hold back a proportion of the general allocation of funding and then distribute this to schools in accordance with estimates of their numbers of children with special needs. These estimates can be based, for example, on tests taken by school entrants or on some demographic measure applied to the schools' catchment areas. Another mechanism, perhaps supplementing the more general estimates, can be to engage in detailed assessments of children thought by teachers and parents to have special needs and to make individual allocations accordingly.

The costs of administering these procedures have to be taken into account, and in the individual allocations it may well be advisable to have some means of monitoring spending, to ensure that the total funds allocated stay within reasonable limits.

Several OECD countries use one or both of these mechanisms. Within the United Kingdom, for example, allocations of funding to schools in recent years as part of an initiative (the Local Management of Schools initiative) designed to enable schools to manage their own finances have involved extra allowance for the proportion of children estimated to have special needs. This runs alongside another mechanism, which has been operating for more than a decade, whereby those children whose special needs are thought to be the greatest are put through a multidisciplinary assessment system (the 'statementing' system); their special needs and the resources required to meet them are expressed in terms of a formal 'statement', which commits the local education authority to providing the education specified.

In practice, as can be seen for example from the report *Special Needs Issues* by Her Majesty's Inspectorate (1990), the statementing system has been found useful but procedures have often been time-consuming, variable from one local authority to another, lacking appropriate consultation with parents, and resulting in vague recommendations. As the expenditure recommended is difficult to forecast and potentially unlimited, local authorities have had problems in managing the uncertainties involved. The government has issued a Code of Practice, which has been implemented since September 1994, and which includes procedures designed to tighten up this system (Department for Education 1994).

SUMMARY

Reports compiled in recent years by Member countries of the OECD are rich sources of information relating to the success or otherwise of inclusive education programmes for children with special educational needs. In this chapter, key issues are presented in three clusters: resources available within regular schools, aspects of school organization, and factors external to schools.

One key issue concerning resources is that of the time needed to introduce innovative programmes and to sustain them. Time is needed for identification of the children to be involved, for consultation among professionals and parents, for assessment of teachers' attitudes and skills, for target-setting to define that which can be achieved, for implementation of the inclusion programmes and of associated in-service education and training, and for evaluation of the work being undertaken. Another key issue is that of the skills involved. It is essential that teachers engaged in the programmes are able to differentiate their teaching sufficiently well to provide effectively for children of different levels of ability in the same class settings, and to do this across the curriculum as a whole, not just in a few subjects.

There are several key issues concerning school organization. For inclusive education to be effective, provision needs to be staged into a continuum, so that children with special educational needs can be helped through various combinations of within-class support, with-drawal group work and individual tuition. Provision of this kind can be co-ordinated through the implementation of a whole-school policy for special needs, whereby all staff agree to share in the responsibilities involved. As more children with special needs are integrated into regular schools, an important feature of the pro-gramme is a constructive approach to handling the reduction in the numbers on roll in special schools. This includes utilizing the existing skills of the teachers employed there and helping them adjust to new roles. Within the regular school, support systems are required to ensure that the teachers concerned develop and sustain the attitudes and skills required for effective working. Effective school organ-ization may extend across schools, with the regular and special schools in a region collaborating to provide a co-operative network of provision and training.

Issues relevant to successful inclusive education extend well beyond the schools themselves. Programmes are more likely to thrive if they are supported by public opinion, and reports provided by OECD Member countries include several examples of good practice in parental and community involvement. An overriding issue is that of funding. While inclusive education programmes need not be expensive, funding mechanisms at local, regional and national levels need to be such as to encourage a shift of emphasis towards special educational provision in regular schools and to facilitate the extra staffing and training required there.

Chapter 8

Inclusion of pupils with learning disabilities in general education settings

Naomi Zigmond and Janice M. Baker

INTRODUCTION

We are in the midst of a revolution in the education of children with disabilities. Historically, special education programmes were developed to protect, nurture, and teach children in whom the presence of a disability made them a burden to general class teachers and vulnerable to failure in school work and to ridicule from classmates. From the outset, the predominant special education strategy was to organize programmes that were segregated by handicapping condition and isolated from the mainstream, on the assumption that such programmes were beneficial. Now, questions are being raised about the efficacy of these segregated placements and about the morality of excluding pupils with disabilities from regular schools. Models of service delivery which seemed logical and appropriate in the past are being challenged. New models are being proposed.

Pupils with learning difficulties (LD) constitute the largest proportion of pupils with disabilities served in special education in the United States and most of them are educated in pull-out programmes in regular schools. Recently, spurred by the Regular Education Initiative (Will 1986), a movement to increase inclusion of pupils with disabilities in educational programmes with non-disabled peers, efforts have been made to return pupils with LD completely to general education classrooms. These experiments in full inclusion of pupils with LD sometimes involve a dramatic reform of the educational experiences provided for all pupils in the school; sometimes they involve only a few volunteer teachers in a very small-scale change process. We have studied models of full inclusion from both ends of this spectrum (see Zigmond and Baker 1995) in an effort to understand how the reform of special education was accomplished and the nature of the educational experiences provided to pupils with LD in these new service delivery models. In this chapter, we will reflect on this American experiment in full inclusion of pupils and on three lessons we learned from that reform initiative: (1) that inclusion should be part of a school-wide reform effort that results in fundamental changes in the philosophy, structure, and curriculum of the regular school; (2) an inclusive school must make available to pupils with LD a continuum of services ranging from self-contained classrooms to full-time placement in the regular class; and (3) the role of the special education teacher is critical to successful inclusive schooling for pupils with LD.

SERVICE DELIVERY MODELS FOR PUPILS WITH LD

Segregated schools

In educating pupils with LD, we, in the United States, have never made heavy use of totally segregated facilities. In the 1991–2 school year, separate day school, residential facility, and hospital or home-bound instruction accounted for only 1.4 per cent of the placements for the more than 2 million pupils designated as LD nationwide (US Department of Education 1993). These very restrictive settings have generally been reserved for those few pupils with LD who require a programme of studies that cannot be provided within a public school attended by children who do not have disabilities. To be paid for out of public coffers, assignments of pupils to these segregated settings must have the agreement of both school officials and parents.

The advantages of separate, restrictive placements are obvious: they serve a very selective clientele and are able to provide alternative, often experimental, programmes to meet pupils' needs. The disadvantages are also obvious: the high expense to the school district or the parents, the travelling distance, and the lack of opportunity to be with other pupils who do not have disabilities for at least some portion of the school day.

Self-contained classes in regular schools

A more common arrangement for educating pupils with LD in the United States is the separate or self-contained class in a regular school. The earliest public school programmes for pupils with LD used this model of service delivery and currently 22 per cent of pupils with LD are served in this way (US Department of Education 1993). The choice of the special class reflects the belief that pupils with LD need a very different sort of school curriculum than their non-disabled peers but that it can be provided in a regular school building; the special class allows pupils with LD to be physically integrated into the school, and to participate in some classes or extra-curricular activities, as appropriate. Enrolments in the special class are kept low (approximately twelve pupils to one teacher) and, when possible, a paraprofessional is assigned to assist the teacher in providing instruction. Teachers have opportunities to restructure both basic skills and content instruction, to integrate across school subjects, to infuse language development and social skills activities throughout the day, and to be more flexible in the scheduling and pacing of lessons.

Research on the effectiveness of special class placements in regular schools, however, has not been encouraging. For example, studies of the learning environments of separate special education classrooms for pupils with LD (see Leinhardt *et al.* 1981) revealed lower cognitive demand, slower paced, more deliberate instruction than one would see in a general education classroom, and surprisingly little time each day devoted to important academic tasks – reading orally or silently, composing written texts, or interacting instructionally with the teacher. But for pupils who need a curriculum different from that offered in the regular class, special class placements satisfy that need.

Resource rooms in regular schools

A less restrictive special education service delivery option is provided by a resource room. Resource room pupils in the United States have a general education classroom as their home base, but they leave that classroom to receive special education programmes and services from a special education teacher for at least 21 per cent but no more than 60 per cent of each school day. Resource room services now constitute the majority of placements (53.5 per cent) of pupils with LD (US Department of Education 1993).

Instruction in a resource room often focuses on basic academic skills – reading, language arts, or mathematics – but might also include direct instruction in learning strategies (Deshler and Schumaker 1988) or survival skills (Zigmond 1990). Resource room time can be devoted to helping pupils complete work that has been assigned to them in their general education classes, or to assisting pupils in taking required tests.

There is some evidence that in resource rooms pupils with LD can make significant progress in academic skill development (Carlberg and Kavale 1980; Madden and Slavin 1983; O'Connor *et al.* 1983). Furthermore, resource room services are not associated with diminished self-concept (Padeliadu and Zigmond, forthcoming; Prillaman 1981) and may even enhance teacher and pupil perceptions of academic progress and personal social adjustment. But despite the apparent success of resource room programmes, they do have some disadvantages: when a pupil is pulled out of one or more general education classes to go to the resource room, he or she must miss whatever is being taught to classmates. Pupils who are already struggling to keep up may be confused by this interruption. Furthermore, pull-out resource room programmes are seldom co-ordinated with the instruction provided in the general education classes, and when resource instruction is supplementary to instruction in the mainstream, there is often little alignment of methods or materials in the two settings. And, if too many pupils are assigned to a resource room at one time, pupils are likely to receive little direct instruction there and be put to work completing worksheets instead.

Full inclusion in general education classrooms

The alternative to the resource room is full-time placement in a general education class, with special services pulled in, rather than the pupil pulled out. Swept along by advocacy groups that consider access to the general education class as a right of all pupils, fomented by legitimate complaints about the rising costs of serving pupils in separate programmes, and in response to growing dissatisfaction about the academic achievement of pupils with LD educated in pull-out settings, school authorities in the United States and elsewhere have sought ways to return pupils with LD to general education classrooms, and to change conditions that lead to referral of pupils for special education services in the first place. Several models of general education service delivery have been developed and field-tested in American schools, particularly at the elementary level (grades K–6, ages 5–11). These models differ widely in how school personnel are selected to participate, how pupils with LD are distributed into general education classes, and how special education is provided.

MODELS OF FULL INCLUSION

Full inclusion as the only option

In Kansas City, Kansas, there is an elementary school that has eliminated all pull-out services for pupils with special needs (for a more complete description see Zigmond 1995a). Knights Elementary School* is an urban school with an enrolment of about 315 pupils; it has two classes at each grade level K–5. There are forty-five pupils in this building assigned to special education services, more than 14 per cent of the pupil population, but this high proportion of pupils with special needs is by design. To make the inclusion model adopted by this school work, they need three special education teachers; that is a legitimate expenditure of school resources only as long as there are about fifteen pupils with special needs per teacher. The principal achieves this high number of labelled pupils by continuing the procedures in the building that lead to identification of pupils with LD, and by recruiting from neighbouring schools pupils who are already identified and labelled. 'If you don't identify them you don't get money for them ... then they're going to come take one of my teachers away', said the Kansas principal (5 March 1993).

Knights is implementing its own variation of a University of Kansas full inclusion model (Reynaud *et al.* 1987) which it has renamed Collaborative Teaching Model (CTM). Seven or eight pupils with LD are assigned as a group to one general education classroom; they constitute approximately one-third of the pupils in that class. The remaining pupils are average or above average achievers. In Knights, one of the two classes at each grade level participates in CTM. One special education teacher has formed a team with one first grade and one second grade teacher; the other two special education teachers collaborate with one third, one fourth, and one fifth grade teacher. A continuum of special education services is not maintained in this building; CTM is all there is for pupils with special needs.

* The schools described here were part of a research study conducted by Zigmond and Baker, described completely in Zigmond and Baker 1995. The names of all the schools, teachers and pupils have been changed to preserve agreements about confidentiality.

CTM classrooms are staffed by a special education teacher and a general education teacher for as much as 3–4 hours each day. Both teachers provide instruction and support to all learners within the class, and both share in all of the scheduled instruction. The teaching teams plan together formally only once a week, but informal planning occurs, on the run, all the time. Planning consists of deciding what will be taught and how it will be taught. There is no discussion of who will be doing the teaching (i.e., of the distribution of responsibilities) since both teachers do everything together, and there is no grouping for instruction.

In CTM classrooms there is a small pupil–teacher ratio and opportunities for all the pupils to interact with adults frequently, but to give a pupil with special needs a little more support, the teachers make extensive use of a 'study-buddy' system, pairing each special needs pupil with a classmate who gives help with assignments as needed. And the teachers adapt the pupils' workloads and use explicit behaviour management systems, as needed.

Full inclusion as school improvement

In Springfield Elementary School in Pennsylvania (PA), the approach to full inclusion is quite different (for a more complete description see Zigmond 1995b). Springfield is a K–6 school with about 460 pupils, nineteen of whom are pupils with LD (4 per cent). The school is implementing MELD, a model of full inclusion developed at the University of Pittsburgh (Zigmond and Baker 1990). It involves all of the teachers in the school (not just half of them) in a total school improvement effort.

Springfield took a full year to prepare for inclusion. Special education teachers attended workshops on co-teaching and consultation. General education teachers received in-service training on classroom management, new ideas on teaching literacy, curriculum-based measurement, progress monitoring, and accommodating pupils with special needs. Most importantly, all the adults in the school discussed the mainstreaming model and how they would be affected by the placement changes.

At Springfield, all pupils with LD, no matter how far behind they are in academic skills, are returned full-time to the mainstream and are distributed across teachers in the building in such a way that no one teacher is particularly burdened. Because it depends on where the pupils with LD fit, some teachers in the building have as many as three pupils with LD in their classroom all day, and others have none. The special education teacher spends full time giving in-class support and co-teaching, giving more time to classrooms into which pupils with LD have been integrated and less time to classrooms that have no pupils with LD. Because there are sixteen classrooms in this school, the most time any one teacher gets is thirty minutes, four times per week. During these co-teaching periods, the two teachers might direct a group together, split the group and each teach the same lesson (reducing class size), or split the group and each teach a different lesson to address different pupil needs.

A regular time is set aside each week for grade-level co-planning meetings: all the classroom teachers of a particular grade level meet with the special education teacher to plan how co-teaching time in each room will be spent. Planning meetings are often scheduled for the half-hour before school opens. The special education teacher views the planning meetings as an opportunity to continue staff development and she comes to each co-planning meeting well prepared. But she is pulled in so many directions that she is frustrated at not having enough time for pupils who are really struggling in the mainstream, 'knowing that you have to walk out of the room and you're letting that teacher be solely responsible for all that attention' (special education teacher, PA, 3 February 1993). Furthermore, the focus of the co-teaching is, of necessity, accommodation not remedial instruction. As the special education teacher describes it, 'Nobody has time to teach these kids [fifth graders] how to read back at their second-grade level. In about two periods a week, I'm not going to teach kids how to read' (3 March 1993).

Guiding the inclusion experiment in Springfield is the belief that if teachers teach their classes well, in ways that make the curriculum accessible to the widest possible range of pupils, the pupils with LD will be able to cope. So, all pupils are taught to use graphic organizers to comprehend text. All pupils have opportunities to work with modified materials (e.g., text-on-tape), modified assignments (e.g., shortened homework assignments in mathematics), and modified tests (e.g., oral exams). And there is a modified grading system so that all pupils in the school have the opportunity to feel successful. But if a particular pupil with LD needs more help than this, parents have to arrange for tutoring before school or after school on a fee-for-service basis, or the pupil has to transfer to another school where a pull-out special education programme is still available; the in-class support programme has used up all of the special education resources available to this school.

Full inclusion with pull-out for anyone

Worthington Elementary School has just over 400 pupils in grades K–6, forty-two of whom are pupils with LD (10.5 per cent) (for a more complete description see Baker 1995b). There are two or three classes at each grade level. The staff at Worthington, with the help of researchers at the University of Washington, designed and implemented a school-building model of inclusion that combines a number of empirically validated elements: a literature-based reading curriculum, cross-age tutoring, co-operative learning, curriculum-based measurement and phonics instruction. Some of these elements are offered outside the general education classroom (e.g., phonics instruction is done in the hallway, and cross-age tutoring takes place in the multi-purpose room). Some pupils also participate in a special instructional group that meets before school, after school, or at lunch-time.

Based on need, any pupil in this school, whether labelled LD or not, can access the special programme available at Worthington. Any pupil might be given an assignment that has been modified in length (e.g., number of spelling words to be learned), response mode (spelling test to be taken orally instead of written), or evaluation criteria (adapted grade for spelling performance). Any pupil can participate in the phonics lessons conducted in the hall every morning. Any pupil might be part of a special instruction group that meets before or after school (extended day) or at lunch-time. And any pupil can receive individual help from peers or participate in co-operative learning groups and class-wide peer tutoring activities in their general education classrooms.

To make this programme work, the special education teacher spends full time providing 'support services'. She organizes and supervises the cross-age tutoring, teaches three of the six phonics groups, leads two of the extended day groups, works with a few individual pupils on an impromptu basis, monitors individual behaviour interventions, and modifies academic assignments. She provides some in-class support to one class at each grade level, though not on a regularly scheduled basis. The special education assistant also takes on significant instructional duties. She teaches the other three phonics groups, directs one of the extended day programmes, and provides in-class support in at least one class at each grade level.

Full inclusion as one option on a continuum of services

Valley Elementary School in Virginia is a very large elementary school of approximately 700 pupils, forty (5.7 per cent) of whom are LD (for a more complete description see Baker 1995a). There are five or six classrooms at each grade level K–5. The collaborative teaching model in this school provides full inclusion only for those twenty-three pupils with LD who are 'ready' to be re-integrated. The remaining pupils with LD receive pull-out instruction in a resource room.

Collaborative teaching is offered in one class at each of third, fourth, and fifth grades; the general education teachers who particip-ate in this full inclusion model volunteered for the assignment. Seven or eight pupils with LD have been placed in each of these classes, all day long. The special education teacher at Valley team-teaches with each of these general education teachers for ninety minutes per day. During this collaborative teaching time, the special education teacher might monitor individual pupils, teach learning strategies to the whole class, teach learning strategies to half the class at a time, or provide one-on-one tutoring. Co-planning is done formally once a week, and informally as needed.

In the Valley model, strategy training is a central component. The special education teacher had received 'Kansas Strategy Training' (Deshler and Schumaker 1988) at the same time that she had begun collaborative teaching; she and her three partners do not think that they are co-teaching if they are not 'doing strategies'. Accom-modating individual pupil needs with adapted materials, assignments, or tests is the second important component of the collaborative teaching model. The special education teacher spends some portion of each day constructing adapted materials and tests.

LESSONS TO BE LEARNED FROM FULL INCLUSION MODELS

Fundamental school reform

It is clear from the American experience that inclusion has different meanings for different people. Inclusion certainly means 'place', a classroom in a regular school building, and a seat in an age-appropriate general education classroom. It also means access to, and participation in, the general education instructional programme, either full-time or part-time. And it means bringing special education teachers or special education paraprofessionals into general education schools and classrooms to help make inclusion work. Beyond this broad conceptualization, however, inclusion can mean very different things in different schools and among different professionals.

But regardless of its precise meaning, in all implementations of more inclusive service delivery models, inclusion that works well is essentially not a reform of special education but a reform of the mainstream. We do not say this to maintain the historic division between general and special education, nor to emphasize the separateness that has characterized relations in the past. Special educators must be part of the ongoing dialogue in general education that will lead to reform of curriculum, school organization, and professional development. Special educators must be part of the team that recreates schools so that all children and youth, among them those with disabilities, might succeed. Curricular reforms in the fields of literacy, mathematics, science, and social studies and the fundamental changes in instructional and assessment strategies that will accompany them must consider the needs of all children who populate the schools, and they will only do so if special educators are integral to the discussions and plans.

The models we have described differ widely with respect to fundamental school reform. For example, in two of the four models, volunteer teachers agreed that as many as one-third of their class could be pupils with special needs; in exchange, the special education teachers assigned to those pupils spent considerable amounts of the school day (between ninety minutes and four hours) co-teaching in those general education classrooms. In the other two models of full inclusion, pupils with LD were dispersed to as many classrooms as possible, so that no single teacher was overburdened by particularly difficult-to-teach pupils; in this case the special education teachers had to limit the amount of time spent co-teaching in each general education classroom because there were more classrooms in which co-teaching had to take place. In both sets of approaches, during those times in the day when there were two teachers in the full inclusion classroom, there was a smaller pupil–teacher ratio so that either of the teachers could give a pupil with special needs a little more support; there were also opportunities for all the pupils to interact with more adults. Inclusive models also made use of peer tutors in formal class-wide peer tutoring systems (as in the Washington Model) or informally as 'study buddies' (as in the Kansas model). Teachers also adapted the pupils' workloads and used explicit behaviour management systems, as needed. But in the first set of models, inclusion represented a change in the way education was offered in a few classrooms in the school building, and change did not reach beyond these few classrooms. In the second set of models, inclusion was part of a total reform of the school; it represented a change in philosophy regarding who was responsible for educating pupils with diverse needs. In the new way of thinking, all pupils belonged in the school and were to be educated by the staff of the school. To accomplish that meant fundamental changes in the curriculum, in the materials, in teaching styles, in assessment, and in grading policies, and the teachers in these buildings had spent considerable time discussing, developing, and implementing these changes.

We believe that inclusion will have lasting meaning and provide an appropriate and successful educational experience for pupils with LD when schools engage in the process of fundamental reform. The likelihood of success is greater when teachers and administrators of regular schools accept responsibility for educating pupils with special needs and responsibility for the changes in curriculum, instructional methods, and policies to undergird it. Some schools may take a full year for their staffs to ready themselves for inclusion; others might accomplish the transformation more quickly. But none does it without some preparation before or during the implementation of changed special education services. That preparation may involve learning new skills or finding new approaches to instruction. But it also involves discussions of the philosophy underlying more inclusive education, the belief that they are responsible for teaching their classes in ways that make the curriculum accessible to the widest possible range of pupils. Inclusion will mean a change in the school climate; it is a statement that a diverse set of learners are not only welcome in the school but will also be accommodated by their teachers.

Some teachers will be won over to the logic of inclusion, by the in-service and planning meetings held before the fact. But regardless of how much preparation is scheduled and how much in-service is provided, other teachers will feel unprepared and apprehensive about the changes that are coming, and no amount of talking will allay their fears. To accomplish change despite these fears, there must be strong and enthusiastic leadership for the inclusion reform, from a teacher, an administrator, or a university consultant. And once the decision is made to move to become a more inclusive school, inclusion should be school policy; it should not depend on finding volunteer teachers who are willing to try it. While we do not question the need for those involved in educating children to believe that the pupils assigned to them are appropriately placed and worthy of investment of time and energy, inclusion reform cannot be accomplished with volunteers. Furthermore, in school-wide reform efforts, we have witnessed changes in attitudes to inclusion that have come about as a result of the experience of educating a pupil with disabilities in a general education setting; active involvement in the inclusion experiment helped to turn negative attitudes into more positive ones (Zigmond 1995b).

Preserving a continuum of services in the regular school

Research evidence on full inclusion models is scant, and the findings are ambiguous. On the one hand, there is a great deal of enthusiasm among the staffs, parents, and pupils themselves about the new models. In full-inclusion schools, pupils with LD are taught enthusiastically, not grudgingly, by general education teachers. Special education teachers, in the roles of co-ordinator, co-planner, and co-teacher, make it possible for general education teachers to feel comfortable about the educational tasks with which they are confronted, and for the pupils with LD in these schools to feel comfortable about functioning in a general education setting. Accommodations are implemented for the entire class, so that from the pupil's perspective s/he is not singled out or made to feel different. Teachers, both general and special, try to teach everyone well, and in that way to meet the needs of the special education pupils who are present (see Zigmond and Baker 1995).

But, in a recent report of three studies, Zigmond *et al.* (1995) describe achievement outcomes for pupils with LD from three full-inclusion models implemented in three parts of the United States (Pennsylvania, Washington, and Tennessee). All three studies utilized the BASS reading subtest as the measure of reading achievement (Espin *et al.* 1989) so that the findings from the three studies could be aggregated and compared. The data suggest that general education settings do not produce desired achievement outcomes for many pupils with LD. The three analyses of reading data indicate that only approximately half of the pupils with LD educated in general education settings made reliable gains in reading achievement, a minority of these children made average-size achievement gains relative to grade-level classmates, around 40 per cent made gains that were less than half the magnitude of the grade-level average, and only approximately half improved their standing in the achievement distribution. By extension, for approximately half of the pupils with LD in the six schools involved in these three studies, achievement outcomes after a year of fully integrated educational programmes and services were unsatisfactory.

Special education has always professed a commitment to providing extra to those in special need. In inclusive schools, pupils with LD have the opportunities to participate in all the same lessons as non-disabled peers. In full inclusion, all educational opportunities for pupils with disabilities are provided in the general education classroom and during the regular school day. Pupils with LD are assigned to homerooms with their non-disabled peers. They cover the age-appropriate curriculum in reading, language arts, mathematics, science, and social studies. They participate in physical education, art, and music with their homeroom group. When holiday and special events occur, they are included with their classmates.

Pupils in these inclusive classrooms use modified materials, assignments, and evaluation tasks, but these accommodations are also available to pupils without disabilities. Teachers shorten assignments (e.g., weekly list of spelling words, number of problems on homework assignment in mathematics) as needed. They provide opportunities for pupils to preview or rehearse next week's reading selections or the next chapter in the science textbook. They are willing to make accommodations for the pupils with LD assigned to their classes, especially if the accommodation can be used for the whole class. Adaptations that fall into this category include re-designed tests, more oral reading of textbooks during class time, allowing any pupil in the class to make use of a mathematics matrix of multiplication or division facts, teaching the entire class some reading or composition strategy, or allowing choice and flexibility in the selection of the weekly spelling list.

But many pupils with LD need more than these accommodations to learn what they need to learn. To make significant progress in academic skill acquisition, some pupils with LD will need specific, directed, individualized, intensive, remedial instruction. Theoretically, this relentless, intensive, alternative educational opportunity could be made available in any venue of a school. But in practice, or at least in the practice of schooling that we have observed, it cannot be accomplished in the general education class. Within the ecology of the general education classroom, where the learning and social interactions of dozens of pupils must be orchestrated, the how of instruction (materials, instructions, structure) can be tinkered with, but the what of instruction (curriculum, pacing) is less amenable to change.

When there is a continuum of services established within the regular school, full inclusion, or in-class special education, is made available for those pupils whose progress in academic skills and social development warrants it. Other pupils, who are not ready for complete integration, will continue to have special education services provided in some other setting from personnel not involved in the in-class efforts. Maintaining two complete sets of services (pull-out and in-class) may be expensive, but it is the only way to ensure that every pupil with LD receives the instructional programmes he or she needs.

In-class services, especially if they are offered school-wide, stretch special education personnel very thin. To economize, schools may opt to use peers, paraprofessionals, and parents in instructional roles that should be assigned to more special education teaching personnel. In the end, the least well-trained individuals are asked to teach the most difficult-to-teach; something certainly to be guarded against!

Pull-out services must also not be delegated to paraprofessionals or peers. These instructional experiences need to be designed to focus on individual pupils and their unique learning needs. The curriculum and instruction must be carefully planned: it must be characterized by intensity and urgency over what needs to be taught and what needs to be learned; it must be relentless and goal-directed; and, it must preserve special education's historic reliance on empirically-validated approaches, demanding evidence of effectiveness, and being critical of popular, bandwagon ideas.

Expanding the role of the special education teacher

In inclusive schools, the special education teacher takes on new roles. The scope of the role reflects both the model that has been selected and the ways in which the particular teacher shapes the role to fit his or her talents and interests. The teacher is responsible for consulting with teachers in general education, and for participating in teacher assistance teams. The teacher teaches pupils with LD and pupils who are not assigned to special education.

One responsibility of the special education teachers in an inclusive school will continue to be to teach pupils with LD. But instruction in the general education setting is not the same as instruction in a special education setting. In the general education setting, the lessons taught by the special education teacher are most likely to be provided to groups consisting of both those with disabilities and non-disabled classmates and the focus will be on the group: managing instruction for a large group of pupils; managing behaviour within a large group of pupils; designing assessments suitable for a large group; etc. During scheduled co-teaching sessions, special education teachers will engage in a wide variety of activities. Sometimes, the two teachers will team-teach a whole-class lesson, with both teachers participating equally in the instructional activity. In this arrangement, there is no differentiation of teacher roles, and for the time that both teachers are present in the room, they are indistinguishable to an observer. An alternative approach to co-teaching involves one of the two teachers teaching a whole-class lesson while the second teacher circulates, monitors, and prompts individual pupils as needed; the two teachers might alternate the role of teacher and monitor. More usually, the class will be divided into two groups with each teacher teaching one of the groups. Sometimes each teacher will teach the same lesson, but having two teachers allows each to teach a smaller group. At other times, the two teachers teach the same objective, but they use different instructional strategies and/or materials. Or, the two teachers each teach a different lesson, but change groups midway through the class period so that all pupils receive both lessons.

In these co-teaching roles, special education teachers may be sensitive about the fact that they are 'guests' in another teacher's class and might be viewed by outsiders (or by their general education partner) as no more than an extra pair of hands, equivalent to a paraprofessional. To avoid being placed in this subservient role, planning time should be built into the schedule. During planning, the special education teacher makes suggestions for ways to infuse learning strategies, or graphic organizers, or a hands-on activity into a lesson that is outlined by the general education teacher. The special education teacher suggests alternative worksheets or assignments both for the lessons s/he might teach and for the ones to be taught by the mainstream teacher. Planning sessions are not only practical: they are also an extension of in-service training for general education teachers.

In an inclusive school, the special education teacher must also be prepared for teaching in a resource room or self-contained class, but we do not mean to suggest a return to the pull-out programmes of the past. Scheduling and excessive case loads have prevented special education teachers from accomplishing their intended purposes. Nevertheless, for some pupils with LD, there are skills and strategies that need to be mastered if instruction in the mainstream is to be meaningful and productive, and these skills and strategies will only be mastered if they are taught explicitly and intensively. In pull-out settings, the lessons will be directed to individuals or very small groups of pupils. The emphasis will be on providing unique and response-contingent instruction; teaching socially appropriate behaviour; designing tailored assessments that are both diagnostic and summative; and so on. The instruction that is delivered will be characterized by opportunities for consistent and sustained time on task; immediate, frequent, and appropriate feedback to the pupils; regular and frequent communication to each pupil that the teacher expects the pupil to master the task and demonstrate continuous progress; and a pattern of interaction in which the teacher responds to pupil initiatives and uses consequences appropriate to the pupil's response. Pull-out settings are more likely to provide these opportunities than full inclusion programmes. Furthermore, short-term, part-time, pull-out programmes also afford a teacher and a pupil the opportunity to engage in intense instruction on objectives that a particular child must learn, that others have already learned, or that others will pick up on their own.

ACHIEVING INCLUSIVE SCHOOLS

No single model of service delivery is best for all pupils with LD, and the research literature which consists primarily of quantitative studies from which authors (ourselves included) report average achievement gains or average changes in social development falls short of providing a roadmap for change. Nevertheless, there are lessons to be learned from the American experience of educating pupils with LD in the regular school. To do it well requires a change in the way the regular school operates. It works best when a continuum of services is available for pupils with LD, since there is no one best way that suits all pupils with special needs. In addition, the special education teacher in an inclusive school must be skilled at working in a wide variety of contexts.

Implementing a more inclusive model of schooling for pupils with special needs requires the will to do it. We know how to reduce referral rates to near zero: by eliminating pull-out options, by making special programmes available to anyone, or by uncoupling supplemental funding mechanisms from placement rates. We know how to provide an adequate general education to pupils with LD: by redeploying special education personnel as support staff to general education teachers and establishing the principle that all children belong in the regular school. There is no 'right' way to proceed with inclusion reform, but with leadership from teachers or administrators inside the school or from outside consultants willing to inspire, instruct, cajole, and support, inclusive schooling can be achieved.

But implementing a better education for pupils with LD will require much more. The schools that we have described invested tremendous amounts of resources, financial and professional, into the enhancement of services for pupils with LD in the mainstream setting. Despite this investment, the achievement outcomes were disappointing. In advocating a change in service delivery for pupils with LD, we must not lose sight of the academic goals that should be set for these pupils, nor can we be satisfied with an educational programme that does not improve literacy and numeracy skills among its benefits. When full inclusion is inadequate to achieve that goal, we must be prepared to reinvent pull-out services and find the resources they will require. There is much to be learned from the American experiment in full inclusion, but the most important lessons may be that inclusion is achievable, inclusion is good, and for some pupils with LD (perhaps as many as half the pupils currently being served in special education) full inclusion is too much of a good thing! We must find a way to balance the values of inclusion with the commitment to teaching individual pupils what they need to learn. Future reform efforts that combine inclusive schooling with the additional resources and specially trained personnel needed to achieve individual educational goals of pupils with LD, in whatever service option is appropriate, might achieve that elusive equilibrium.

Chapter 9

Restructuring special education provision

Cor J. W. Meijer and Luc M. Stevens

INTRODUCTION

When the aim of a government's policy to integrate special and regular education is measured according to the number of children being taught in an integrated setting, we must conclude that the Netherlands has not been particularly successful in this field. Though, of course, the idea of integration needs to convey more qualitative connotations (Pijl and Meijer 1991), policy and practice have failed thus far to educate children with special needs in regular schools. This is especially the case for the children in schools for the learning disabled (the so-called LOM schools) and in schools for mildly mentally retarded children (MLK schools). These two school types cover about 70 per cent of all children in separate special schools. In this chapter we confine ourselves to the situation of children in these special schools. A discussion of the necessary resources required for integrated education, the conditions in class and school which need to be met, as well as external school factors, can be enhanced not only by carefully analysing factors that make for success, but also by examining attempts at integration that were unsuccessful. Without any intent to label negatively various successful local and regional developments and inevitably from a highly generalized standpoint, the Dutch situation with its segregated system is particularly relevant to the debate.

The following sections closely examine the essential factors that are responsible in the Netherlands for the lack of success in integrating special and regular education. The next section outlines recent Dutch views concerning the lack of success in integrating special and mainstream education. The questions are whether these are valid views and whether there is a scientific basis for them, which objectives and resources are felt necessary in order to turn the tide in favour of the current aim of integration in the Netherlands, and which recent developments exist as a result of the government's new integration policy. The chapter concludes with a short assessment of what is felt to be one of the most essential conditions in any process of integration: the perception of the teacher.

ANALYSIS OF THE PROBLEM

Recent analytical thinking on the factors that have contributed to an expanding special education system can be traced to a large number of studies on the subject (among others, Doornbos and Stevens 1987, 1988; Meijer *et al.* 1993). The factors are broadly divided into three groups (Ministerie van Onderwijs en Wetenschappen 1990, 1991). First, there are various policy and administrative conditions that contribute to segregation, the most important of which is that until recently certain regulations actually encouraged the expansion of a separate special education system. There are two separate laws, one for regular education and one for special education. At the same time, government legislation aimed at integration, such as the start-up of regional projects designed to stem the flow of pupils attending special schools, did not have the desired effect. Where there were results, these did not go beyond the project concerned: there was no dissemination of what had been learned or it had little effect. Other measures like those aimed at increasing the expertise of teachers in regular schools were unsuccessful or produced the opposite effect – such as an increase in referrals partly due to the fact that pupils' problems were identified earlier.

The second group concerns educational factors. In analysing the problem here much support was gained from Doornbos and Stevens's studies (1987, 1988) into the background of the increase in special education. These suggest that there is an imbalance between what a school can provide and the demands made on it by parents and society. Mention is also made of the fact that education does not sufficiently take into account the increasing differences among pupils. There is the general feeling that the school population has become more difficult to teach, while failure is becoming increasingly less acceptable (by parents and teachers). Finally, there are no special facilities available for children who are 'different' in regular schools, which results in more referrals to special education where more time and specialist knowledge are available.

The third group concerns the effects of the existence of two separate systems. This division has several negative consequences: the help required is inextricably linked to a special education setting, which largely results in pupils being placed permanently in separate schools with all the attendant disadvantages. Special education is also an attractive alternative as it provides for extra help.

VALIDITY OF THE PROBLEM

The fact that the Dutch government policy on integration has been unsuccessful is demonstrated by the expanding special education sector. Moreover, the many assessments of government policy on integration, in the sense of the evaluation of the development of special needs facilities in regular primary schools, convey the same clear message. The most prominent measures introduced by the government, such as the introduction of local experiments, the opportunities for peripatetic supervision (or ambulant teaching) and large-scale in-service training, have not led to a reduction in the number of special education referrals. The 1985 Primary Education Act (Ministerie van Onderwijs en Wetenschappen 1985) – which aimed, among other things, to achieve a continuous development and to take differences in pupils' abilities, interests and learning pace into account – was not enough to halt the number of children being referred to special schools.

Thus, the ineffectiveness of government policy is a fact that is simple to establish. More interesting are the questions of why it failed to create a U-turn and whether the policy itself contributed to an increase in special education referrals.

It is worth considering the 'paradox of legislation' (Doornbos 1991; Van Rijswijk 1991). Doornbos and Van Rijswijk suggest that the government, while promoting integration, is in fact rewarding the increase in special education. In other words, the government inadvertently stimulates what it does not want. Funding is not linked to pupils but depends on the type of education they receive. In practice, this means that the government rewards every referral to a special school. Maintaining children with special needs in regular schools or arranging their return from the special to the regular school is insufficiently encouraged. Thus, with the current system a premium is put on segregation, while integration is 'punished'. Next to these incentives there are other, more immaterial, disadvantages, which Doornbos describes (1991). Education policy contributes to the attractiveness of having a separate special education system by portraying its schools as being first-rate remedial teaching institutes where intensive specialist help is available. This also leads to a sustaining of our segregated education system. As a result, parents and teachers meet the strong suggestion that special schools have the requisite expertise and provision for expert, individual and intensive remedial care, while regular schools do not provide anything. Such a viewpoint hardly promotes keeping children with special learning needs in regular education. What is more, parents and teachers feel that primary schools wait too long before referring. Furthermore, when teachers refer pupils with special needs to special education, they are left with a more homogeneous class of pupils to teach. Teachers also admit that this is one of the benefits (Knuver and Reezigt 1991). In other words, they wish to keep their pupils' learning progress as far as possible at the same level.

The problem also refers to the increasing pupil differences and therefore to a heavier workload in primary education as well as to the impossibility of schools taking these differences properly into account. Indeed, there are certain trends that seem to support this. For instance the number of ethnic minority pupils has increased and some of these pupils are seriously behind in the Dutch language. Furthermore, the number of medically vulnerable children increases due to improved care (Orlebeke *et al.* 1990). There are already huge differences in achievement and development in the infant classes. Some four-year-olds, for instance, have skills comparable to other six-year-olds (Van Kuyk 1990).

Special attention should be given to the problem of the inability of regular schools to take differences among pupils into account. The widespread approach in Dutch schools is that all children are expected to learn the same material in precisely the same amount of time. The curriculum allows little room for differences in learning rate, aptitude and level. Differentiation is confined to extremely narrow boundary lines and hardly ever goes beyond the boundaries of that particular class (Reezigt and Weide 1989). As a result, having to repeat a year has not yet disappeared from Dutch primary schools. According to Knuver and Reezigt (1991) over 90 per cent of primary schools still use this measure and between 1 and 2 per cent of children have to repeat a class each year. It seems that particularly within the early learning process, schools are unable to deal with differences among pupils. Teachers specifically point out that repeating a year is a tool for creating homogeneous classes. Pupil differences seem to pose huge problems for primary education and the only way these can be reduced is by taking drastic action in the form of pupils repeating years and referrals to special education.

One of the consequences of separate special and regular education seems to be the emphasis on pupil characteristics. The assessment procedure (which is done by admission boards connected to special schools) generally confirms the opinion of teachers and parents that there is 'something wrong' with the child (Doornbos 1991). The decision-making process is highly subjective: similar groups of pupils can be found in both special and regular education. There is considerable overlap between pupils who are placed in special schools and those who are not (Pijl and Pijl 1993). Currently, the system of admission boards is coming under increasing criticism.

It also appears that referral to a special school is usually permanent. Only a tiny minority (less than 1 per cent) of pupils with special needs in LOM and MLK schools return to regular primary education in any year (Centraal Bureau voor de Statistiek 1993).

The question is, to what extent special schools (for the mild special needs categories, LOM and MLK) differ from regular schools. Researchers have found many similarities concerning teaching methods, teacher behaviour and organization (Pijl and Pijl 1993; Van Rijswijk 1986). There are huge differences within schools, but it is difficult to trace obvious differences between school types. This is also confirmed by the teachers themselves (Doornbos 1991; Doornbos and Stevens 1987): certain special schools are quite similar to regular schools and vice versa.

The problem of the growth of the special school system is also aggravated by doubts about the effectiveness of special education. Span (1988) studied the nature and effectiveness of education provision among similar groups of pupils in regular, LOM, and MLK schools. He concluded that there are great differences within school types (large discrepancies within special and within regular education), but there are no differences between school types. Education provision is more or less the same in LOM, MLK, and primary schools. Broadly speaking, the same education provision is possible in primary as well as in special education, although Span mentions the enormous differences within both special and regular education. He concludes that instruction time is the important factor in accounting for differences in achievement (Span 1988).

Almost no research has been conducted on the long-term effects of special education referrals, for instance on secondary school career or job prospects. The research that has been done (Drenth and Meijnen 1989) reveals that ex-special education pupils have some disadvantage in the labour market.

Finally, it can be concluded that the problem is a sufficiently valid one. In particular, the importance of incentives needs to be stressed. Special education referral is attractive for virtually all concerned. It is difficult, however, to assess its advantages and disadvantages for pupils. All indications point to the proposition that at the very least it is possible for many children with special needs to be taught in regular schools with the same results as in a separate special education setting.

FROM PROBLEM TO PERSPECTIVE

In the Netherlands, the perspective of integrating special and regular schools is defined by the concept of 'adaptive education'. This concept in fact forms the educational core of recent government policy on integration, which is promoted under the slogan 'Together to school again'. This integrative policy aims to offer special provision for more children with special needs within regular schools through various measures. By transferring the facilities and resources of special education more readily to regular schools and by having schools working together on integration, the government is seriously attempting to achieve integration. A first step towards this was to establish regional school clusters of both regular and special schools. There are also plans to review financial policy whereby the ultimate aim is to transfer parts of special education funding to regular schools.

The teachers in regular schools should themselves be aware that teaching within mainstream education generally will need to provide more individual education, in particular for children with special needs. Who are these children? Many researchers have established the relative nature of the criteria according to which these children are defined (Doornbos 1971; Maas 1992; Meijer 1988; Posthumus 1947; Stevens 1987). Teachers refer pupils who are behind in learning within the context of a class situation. There is no generally applied norm against which children are measured; it is much more a teacher-related standard based on the degree to which the teacher is able to cope with differences in the classroom.

Adaptive education takes differences between pupils into account. The teacher's role in this is essential. High demands are made on his/her competency as a teacher, so that this type of education is not only a matter of provisions such as special classes, remedial teaching, resource rooms, and so on. Obviously, provisions play an important role but the prime concern here is the changes within the actual teaching process, initiated and implemented by the teachers, which accommodate the differences in abilities and aptitudes among pupils. In this context, Stevens (1987) stresses the importance of the teacher's perspective. The concern should be with providing not only teaching and technological adjustments but also relational and motivational ones (Van Werkhoven *et al.* 1987a, 1987b). In the last section we will return to this issue.

As mentioned before, two main approaches are now available as a result of recent government integration policy: school clusters and a reassessment of the funding system. The clusters consist of one or more special schools working with a larger group of primary schools. In the last few years the clusters have been implemented. This has resulted in a nationwide network in which every special and regular school is attached to a cluster. While schools were given a certain degree of freedom in the way they were grouped, the aim was that fifteen regular schools would work co-operatively with one special education school (based on the current provision level of 8,000 regular primary schools and 500 LOM and MLK schools). Recent findings, however, show considerable deviation from this. Most affiliations comprise thirty schools on average, including two special schools. The number of pupils involved also varies enormously: from over 10,000 per cluster to less than 500. Extra funding was available to set up these clusters. The resources each cluster receives depend on the number of 'ordinary' pupils and the number of special education schools: Dfl 28 per pupil and Dfl 5,000 per special school. Thus an 'ideal' cluster (3,000 primary school pupils and a special school) receives Dfl 90,000, earmarked for more provision for children with special needs.

The second approach to encourage integration is to introduce a new funding structure. The idea of this new system is that almost half of the special education funds will be allocated to the school clusters. This allows for variation in the way in which integration is carried out. School clusters may decide to maintain the special provision in special schools. They could also decide to transfer parts of that provision to regular schools in one way or another. A key point is the fact that regular schools participate in the decision-making process concerning the structure of special provisions.

The question remains as to the extent to which these two main means will foster the government objective of integrating special and regular education. The setting up of school clusters will not directly result in adaptive education. Much more is needed. However, it must be said that without the necessary facilities (in terms of extra specialist help/time/attention) adaptive education has little chance of succeeding. In this sense, introducing a new funding structure is one of the necessary preconditions for integration. And when introducing a new funding system, the setting up of school clusters is also a necessary prerequisite. Generally, primary schools are too small to arrange effective provision for children with special needs on their own (Wedell 1994). From this viewpoint, school clusters can be identified as a precondition for achieving adaptive education. A new funding structure is a logical and necessary second step.

REVIEW OF THE PRESENT SITUATION

What conclusions can be drawn about the sort of conditions that positively influence an integration policy? To answer this, we need to distinguish conditions at the teaching and system levels as well as those related to school clusters, legislation and funding.

It is extremely important that teachers are motivated enough to educate all their pupils, including those with special needs. Teachers should also be able to cope with differences among pupils: in other words, provide adaptive education. In this sense, the average pupil should not be the starting-point for teaching behaviour. It is also essential that teachers reflect on their own behaviour when dealing with pupils with special needs and time should be set aside for this. Teachers themselves should stay responsible for educating children with special needs, even if this is temporarily done by a teacher assistant or a remedial teacher. To achieve the aforementioned, teacher training should aim at active acceptance of individual differences among pupils and at acquiring skills to deal with differing abilities and a positive attitude towards differences among children. Separate training for regular and special education encourages the tendency to refer pupils to separate systems.

The curriculum should cover the same activities for both children with special needs and their peers, but at the same time the curriculum should facilitate different approaches of teaching, different pace in learning and different levels of achievement (Hegarty 1994). Differences within the classroom should not lead to a negative assessment of the learning process, such as pupils having to repeat a year.

As has become clear, it should come as no surprise that having a separate system for regular and special education impedes the integrating of children with special needs. More importantly, it encourages referrals. The notion that special help, attention, or any other course of action goes hand in hand with referral to a segregated school is outdated and crude, especially when it invariably means that children are being removed from their environments and their peers. The child should not be taken to the facilities, but the facilities should be brought to the child.

Special education schools need to adapt themselves into resource centres to support primary school teachers, develop new materials, gather and disseminate information, provide in-service courses and counsel parents and children. In short, special provision is transferred to regular education and the (smaller) special school can play a supporting role.

We can be brief about the role school clusters can play. A decentralized approach, resulting in the development and implementation of local/regional forms of provision, seems an important condition. It stimulates local/regional involvement and also allows for the necessary degrees of freedom in the way provisions are integrated into regular schools (Meijer *et al.* 1994). In this context it is necessary that school clusters really do have the tools, such as administrative powers and proper funding, to put various integration ideas into practice.

Separate legislation for regular and special education is an important factor in creating a segregated system. It underlines the legislator's view that pupils with special educational needs should be placed in special schools. One act for primary education is a vital condition for achieving integrated education. Also the specific rules and regulations need to be assessed against current thinking that pupils with special needs should be educated in regular schools. Statutory procedures should not impede any progress towards integrating special and mainstream education.

Funding is a further key factor in integration. The way in which financial resources are allocated can positively influence integration (OECD 1995a). If policy is not translated properly into financial terms, then it has little success of being implemented. In other words, if the government proclaims integration, it has to be clearly arranged in a financial sense: there should be a distinct integration incentive.

Connecting financial resources to a separate system is a clear victory for segregationism and results in more children being placed outside the mainstream.

There are two possible financial models here. The first ties resources to pupils (for example through a 'voucher system'). No matter where a pupil is educated, the resources follow the pupil. This appears to have certain disadvantages. It can result in time-wasting, bureaucratic registration procedures and the unnecessary labelling of children. Moreover, it can attract more children to special needs provision.

The second model is based on allocating resources on the basis of the number of pupils within a certain area or region, regardless of the number of children who have special educational needs (the 'budget system'; Meijer *et al.* 1995). This is based on the premise that there are no large regional differences regarding the frequency of educational problems. In fact this model is also based on the conviction that any difference in the number of pupils with special needs is largely determined by the level of provision. Funds can be allocated to a cluster of schools which then decide how the funds are to be used. The funds can also be used to finance any separate special provision. In this case more funds for special schools result in less funds for integrated care.

THE ROLE OF THE TEACHER: CONDITIONS AND PERSPECTIVES

In the foregoing, various aspects were mentioned that are seen as relevant to achieving the goal of integrating pupils with special needs into regular schools. Obviously it is not only important where such pupils are educated but also the standard of provision they receive. This concluding section touches on one aspect that can be seen as determining the quality of integration: the teachers.

Any debate on educational innovation is linked to the views of the key persons, the teachers. It is how they see their role and responsibilities, their perceptions and experience, that affects the success of educational reform. They are the most important intermediaries of the education process. It is a paradox therefore that, in the Netherlands at least, teachers generally leave discussions about educational reform, including integration, to others. An example of this is that in the Netherlands regular schools hastily began appointing internal support teachers to promote the teacher's new role. There is also the example of Dutch polytechnics appointing quality control managers at the moment the government began making these institutes more accountable for standards. The fact that such new appointments can be a support to teachers is not disputed, but it should be a warning that teachers regard educational reform as something to be achieved by others.

Examples like these make it obvious that, if integration between regular and special schools is to succeed, teachers need to start seeing themselves as also being potentially capable of implementing new ideas, and that increasing competence in this is in their own personal interest. This precondition at the same time represents the perspective from which integration should be viewed: namely, professionalization which also contains an emancipatory element for teachers and education. This proposition will be further elaborated upon by further defining the four preconditions for successful integration. First, the objective of 'integration' should be replaced by the objective of 'developing good education'. Second, pupils should not be defined as the object of education, but as subjects in the education process. Third, teachers should direct the development of good education themselves within a process of self-professionalization. Fourth, teachers should learn to see each other as the most important sources of support and therefore should share rather than delegate responsibilities.

Clarifying integration in terms of good education is based on the assumption that pupils will accomplish learning tasks according to their own talent, pace and temperament. If teaching is to be effective here, this means it takes into account differences in pupil characteristics and needs. This fundamental principle, which is based on the nature of child development, is now only realized to a limited extent. Teaching is generally organized on the basis of similarities between pupils and on fixed expectations derived from what a certain age group generally achieves. This situation creates a more or less stable percentage of casualties (Doornbos 1969, 1987; Stanovich 1986). A relevant example of this rigid attitude is that in the Netherlands all pupils who enter grade three of the regular school in August are expected to read and write by Christmas. The teaching of pupils who do not live up to academic expectations is from the teachers' perspective seen as an extra chore. They regard integration in the same way: it is something over and above the 'usual' work, an additional duty.

This view is obviously not in accordance with the natural existing differences among pupils. Practically speaking, there is a limit to the range of individual differences with which a teacher can cope. Recognizing this, however, should not prevent a school questioning what they are doing or whether the way they define their pupils' development is the right one. Such reflection on the part of school and staff requires taking the pupils' perspective on the way they educate. We are inclined to regard the ability of teachers to take this perspective as essential for professionalism within education, just as essential as it is in child rearing. In 1985 Dutch legislation (Primary Education Act) expressed this desired shift in thinking in education by stating that schools should provide 'continuous' education for every pupil, reckoning with individual differences in development.

The second condition – the need for pupils to be seen less as the object of education and more as subjects – directly relates to the first in the sense that they are 'active agents' striving for fulfilment of basic psychological needs of self-determination, competency and the forming of relationships (deCharms 1976; Deci and Chandler 1986; Deci and Ryan 1985). It is these areas that motivate them. Cognitive literature has highlighted the importance of the motivational element in education and learning (Ames and Ames 1984, 1985, 1989). Learning is action par excellence. It presupposes targeted and strategic mental behaviour, awareness and intention, qualities which presume a certain motivational status (Stevens 1994). Pupils are not therefore 'responding systems' (Berliner 1989: 318).

Children with persistent problems in learning, however, have been defined as inactive learners (Borkowski *et al.* 1989; Torgesen 1977). Things happen to them in school, and there is too little active involvement and self-awareness. There seems to be no conscious control in the way they interact with their environment or in problem-solving. This is also connected to a predictable lack of motivation to make an effort to do anything which is seen as being unattainable and which evokes no feelings of competency (Stevens 1994). As is already known, teachers respond to the behaviour that accompanies this attitude (inattention, restlessness and evasion) with increasing control or repeating and variously changing instructions. Instead of looking at the situation from the pupils' perspective and attempting to stimulate their initiatives, teachers remain locked in a stimulus–response model. This creates disappointing results. We can establish here that what children need first and foremost creates a paradoxical situation as far as current education is concerned. Instead of an adequate response to the basic psychological needs of auto-

nomy, self-determination, competency and relationships that children who stay behind require, schools provide an exaggerated
dependency, a lack of competency (due to the system of relative
assessment) and charged relationships with teachers and peers.

As far as the third condition is concerned – the teacher as a
'director' of educational reform – innovation literature consistently
refers to the importance of teachers' personal endorsement and
adoption of educational innovations (Fullan 1982; Joyce and Showers
1988; Van den Berg and Vandenberghe 1988). The teacher is no
longer a 'responding system' and studies on teacher thinking are
convincing about this (Calderhead and Gates 1993; Clark and
Petersen 1986; Day *et al.* 1990; Good and Brophy 1994; Rudduck
1983). Literature also reveals how stable or relatively unsuggestible
teachers' cognitive processes are. On a day-to-day basis teachers have
to be in control of an extremely complex reality. If they are relatively
successful in this, then they are reluctant to change views and
behaviour to which this can be attributed. Thus proposals for
change must not only be personally accepted by them but should
also be in their own personal interest. In the introduction to this
concluding section, we described this interest in the form of experiencing an increased competency. Within the context of integration, this means in concrete terms that teachers have the feeling they
are dealing with pupils' behaviour and motivational problems more
effectively than before. This experience can be generated through the
teachers themselves, with the help of a support system which enables
them to systematically analyse, examine and provide solutions to
problems experienced in the classroom (Calderhead and Gates 1993;
Hopkins 1993; Stenhouse 1983); in other words, an operational
approach, backed up by a system that supports teachers' assessment
procedures into gaining an insight into their own situation on both
a cognitive and behavioural level. Successful attempts to reach
predetermined goals using one's own strength increase feelings of
competency and professional satisfaction. Not unimportant here is
that in this way accountability is possible on the basis of assessment
data generated by the teachers themselves. Thereby education can
gradually acquire what until now has been largely missing: well-
founded reasoning. The quality of the support system will be
extremely important, especially the feedback element, which brings
us to the last of our proposed preconditions.

As a fourth condition, we suggested that teachers learn to see
their colleagues as the most important resource. In an influential

publication on the most effective ways and means of improving special needs provision, Will (1986) suggests a distance as short as possible between the place where the teacher has to resolve problems and the necessary resources to do this. Ideally, this means resources should be available within the school and the most powerful of these are fellow teachers. This is not only because teachers learn most easily from other teachers, but because it represents one of the most effective ways of learning: direct feedback. A prerequisite for such a favourable situation is that teachers feel jointly responsible for developing expertise and problem-solving within their school. As we have already stipulated, here too a greater degree of awareness and initiative is required of teachers.

The arguments above suggest preconditions for successfully integrating children with special needs into regular schools. These proposals have inevitable anthropological implications because a new approach towards the concept of development and the pupil as an individual is required. A new approach also involves the profession of the teacher. Typical qualities related to professionalism, namely competence and autonomy in the work one is doing, will partly take on a new meaning. The aim is to have a profession which is open to criticism and which strives to be accountable within a continuous process of professionalization. This evokes and hopefully results in a more emancipatory perspective for education. It comes down to the self-concept of education, as it presents itself to society, the self-concept of the school, and the self-concept of the teacher.

SUMMARY AND CONCLUSIONS

Various conditions contribute to the segregation of children with special needs in the Netherlands. Until recently certain regulations actually encouraged the expansion of a separate special education system. The special provision is linked to a special education setting, which results in pupils being placed permanently in separate schools. Maintaining children with special needs in regular schools was insufficiently encouraged. As a result, parents and teachers accede to the suggestion that special schools have the expertise and provisions, while regular schools do not provide anything. Such a viewpoint discourages the maintenance of children with special needs in regular education.

Recent integration policy, focusing on the learning disabled and the mildly mentally retarded, has resulted in two new approaches. The first is the implementation of school clusters. This has led to a nationwide network in which every special and regular school is attached to a cluster. The second instrument to encourage integration is to introduce a new funding structure. Costs for special education will be partly allocated to the school clusters. The question is whether this will foster the government objective of integrating special and regular education. In our view, school clusters and the new funding structure are indeed necessary preconditions for integration. But teachers are the key persons who determine the quality of integration. Integration is equivalent to good education in which pupils should not be defined as the object of education, but as subjects in the education process. Teachers should direct the development of good education themselves within a process of self-professionalization and they should learn to see their colleagues as the most important sources of support.

Chapter 10

Structuring the curriculum for pupils with learning difficulties

Developing schools as cultures

*Peter Evans**

INTRODUCTION

Successfully integrating pupils with special educational needs (SEN) into regular schools requires many changes within and outside the school. However, whatever else is achieved, functional integration of disabled pupils into the regular classroom life of the school will not be achieved without modifications being made to the curriculum and to pedagogy. This inevitably means the creation of new teaching resources for the children concerned.

This rather straightforward statement of the problem is, however, difficult to achieve in practice and requires collaboration between the various actors in the school and support from the political and administrative sources outside the school which make up the educational system (OECD 1995a). Furthermore, there is a need for everyone to accept that the problem of supporting disabled pupils in mainstream schools is a problem of the whole school making the necessary adaptations to meet the needs of the pupils and not the pupils having to adapt to the uncompromising demands of the school. A key component of this thinking is that all students are on a continuum of learning ability. That is, from an educational perspective no qualitative distinction is made between the disabled and the non-disabled.

Thus, in making the conceptual leap from an administrative categorization of pupils into various types of disability groups to the educational conception of SEN, there is a need to formulate an educationally relevant understanding of the problem. This should link an understanding of the learning problems experienced by

* The chapter represents the views of the author only and cannot be interpreted to reflect those of the OECD or any of its Member countries.

children with SEN to processes of schooling. The task requires a return to basic principles and in the following text an attempt is made to provide a possible account. It is based largely on the fuller account given in Evans (1988). This chapter focuses in particular on the largest group of SEN pupils, those children with learning difficulties.

THEORETICAL FRAMEWORK

Overview

Since the unfolding of the argument is complex, it is worth beginning by first providing a brief overview of the main theoretical elements and assumptions. These will then be expounded at greater length and the relevance to integration, in the context of curriculum development, clarified. It is important to bear in mind at the outset that any such description must be essentially socio-cognitive, goal-directed and systemic in nature. This last point means that it must take account of three interdependent levels of development: the child, the classroom and the school.

Thus, in overview the argument is first that learning is a social process. To a very large degree all children take on the structure of the knowledge that is transmitted to them by their schools through their teachers in both the open and the hidden curriculum.

Second, learning is about structuring knowledge. Since the acquisition of knowledge implies its structuring by the child, it follows that increased difficulties in learning will at least in part be related to increased difficulties in structuring knowledge.

Third, the implications for those with learning difficulties are that the greater the learning difficulty the child is experiencing, the more the teacher must act as a mediator between the child and his environment to compensate for these difficulties. It then follows, from the second and third points above, that the adjustments that the teacher makes should represent an attempt to transact the curriculum in such a way as to allow the child the opportunity to abstract mutually acceptable learning and knowledge.

Fourth, an organizational approach is required. In the course of their schooling, children will be taught by more than one teacher in many different curriculum areas. The child's education can never be achieved through only one teacher but must reflect a whole-school approach in which all members of the staff are involved in the development of agreed goal-directed, problem-solving strategies. In order for this to work, there needs to be a structuring of this whole environment or system, that is through the development of the curriculum, its pedagogy and its organization. In this way children's special learning needs can in principle be met.

Learning as a social process

The first part of the argument is a rather uncontentious one, namely that learning is a social process. There are a number of sources which can be used to support this view and which are relevant to education. Explanations must be concerned with how children gain access to knowledge and its explicit and implicit meanings as well as to other features of the school curriculum. Mead (1934) argued forcefully that the development of both mind and the self was based on the medium of language. The establishment of meaning requires two loci, the speaker and the spoken to, and it develops an equivalence for the two actors in the course of their interaction. Wood (1980), working within a constructionist paradigm, speaks of children's learning being 'structured through social interaction' (238), and later there is 'increasing internalisation both of mentally represented actions on the physical world, and perspectives and dialogues derived from the social world' (241).

Vygotsky (1978) has been perhaps the most influential theorist. He believes that learning cannot be separated from the socio-historical practices and the teacher's role is to draw children forward into an understanding of culture through engagement with the zone of proximal development (ZPD). Vygotsky proposed that human learning presupposes a specific social nature and a process by which children grow into the intellectual life of those around them. Specifically this occurs through the ZPD. There are two aspects involved: any function appears twice on the scene in the cultural development of the child, on two levels, first the social and then the psychological, first among people, then within the child himself (ibid.). This is Vygotsky's second fundamental psychological law. This law is manifested particularly in the domain Vygotsky called the zone of proximal development.

The general sense of this 'zone' is that at a certain stage in a child's development, a child can resolve a particular range of problems only under the guidance of adults and in collaboration with more intelligent comrades, but cannot do so independently. Thus pedagogy should be oriented not towards yesterday but towards tomorrow in child development. Only then will it be able to create, in the process of education, those processes of development (Vygotsky 1978).

These arguments support what is perhaps self-evident. There can be little doubt that school learning is in large part a social process in which children are introduced to ways of thinking and acting which are acceptable to the culture concerned and that communication mainly in the form of language and literacy is crucial for this process and for the development of knowledge.

Learning is about the structuring of knowledge: schooling is about fostering structuring

If learning is interpreted within the information-processing paradigm, then there can be little doubt that learning is an active process in which information on being learned is interpreted in the light of the learner's knowledge structures. Since the learner has a limited capacity (Kahneman 1973) all aspects of learning are of necessity a small selection of what is available. Various writers have recognized the importance of structuring information for simplification, for the generation of new propositions and for the increased manipulability of a body of knowledge. One aspect of this process at work has been called 'automatization'. Here a skill which at first occupies much of the available limited capacity becomes automatic through practice thereby requiring less conscious awareness in its performance and freeing capacity for new learning or attention.

Implications for children with learning difficulties

If children with learning difficulties are weak or slow in the ability to organize, structure or automatize information, then there will be a downwardly spiralling effect on the child's future cognitions and potential development over time (Evans 1986). This is because material that would connect with existing cognitive networks may fail to do so and thus be treated as 'new' and correspondingly meaningless to the child. In this way incoming information is not simplified through the extraction of commonalities or made sensible. Herriot et al. (1977) demonstrated that children with severe learning difficulties did not cluster items in memory as extensively as their non-disabled peers. Cromer (1986) has also demonstrated that special school pupils with moderate learning difficulties have more immature linguistic structures available to them for abstracting meaning from simple sentences.

Another educationally relevant aspect of this feature of the functioning of children with learning difficulties is difficulty in the transfer of learning: a topic of considerable importance in education. Indeed, transfer is so central that some authors (e.g., Ferrara *et al.* 1986) have argued that a failure to transfer learning is not only indicative of learning difficulty but is one of the defining features. Putting this another way, in the framework of information processing, the ability to transfer learning comes through the development of rules and concepts which themselves are a product of the structuring of knowledge by the learner.

Ferrara *et al.* (1986) have investigated aspects of the relationship between teaching and the transfer of learning within the Vygotskian framework. These authors provide an operational definition of the ZPD as 'an inverse function of the number of prompts that children need both in achieving successful independent performance within a problem domain and subsequently in maintaining and transferring their acquired knowledge to increasingly different problem types' (Ferrara *et al.* 1986).

Children with wide proximal zones are efficient learners in a particular domain: they can capitalize on a relatively small amount of aid. Children with narrower zone widths, in contrast, tend to require much more intervention. This outcome was supported by a number of empirical studies on the transfer of inductive reasoning rules.

Children's learning of a particular curriculum area can be regarded as varying along a continuum of activity. Thus for any particular child learning an aspect of the curriculum, his/her total learning capacity may be characterized by representing high ability as a high level of active involvement and low ability as a low level of active involvement. Other factors are the transfer of learning and rule abstraction. Commensurate with this description are implications that there needs to be a high level of structured teaching input for those with low levels on these factors, but a lower level of structured input for those at the other end of the continuum.

The job, then, for schools is to structure their curriculum appropriately through curriculum and organizational development. The more effectively this is done the better will the school be able to cope and fewer pupils will fail, be identified as having learning difficulties and be segregated. Thus the structure of knowledge that children learn through their active engagement with their teachers and the curriculum area is a reflection of the structure of the knowledge that is transmitted. As pupils experience increasing difficulties with learning, that is their ability to create this structure for themselves is relatively limited, then the structure that is transmitted must be made correspondingly more clear and linked more closely to the pupil's own personal experience. For these reasons teachers, too, need to develop a clearer understanding of the structure of the curriculum subjects in order to be able to teach those experiencing difficulties more effectively. This can be achieved by appropriate organizational development within the school.

An organizational approach – the educational context

So how can this development be achieved in a way that is sensitive to cost issues? There is, of course, more than one answer to this question. However, in brief it is likely that ultimately the most effective solution will prove to be to treat the school as a culture in its own right and to use an action research methodology to develop a progressive response, derived from the school itself, to those children who are having difficulties. Such an approach would strengthen the school base and decrease dependence on external support (e.g., see Fullan 1991a). This approach can be illustrated by referring to some work on curriculum development for children experiencing learning difficulties carried out by Evans *et al.* (1988), Ireson *et al.* (1989, 1992) and Redmond *et al.* (1988).

Following analysis of documentation and interviews with head-teachers and staff in thirty schools, selected as representing 'good practice', key aspects of the functioning of the schools said to be successful in education of children with learning difficulties, were identified.

The main components have been put together in a model intended to represent a co-ordinated system which has the classroom at its core. Figure 10.1 is a simplified model of school-based curriculum development in special education. The figure shows some of the interrelationships of categories of data in the curriculum development process for children with special educational needs. The model is intended to represent a co-ordinated, interdependent and hierarchical system which has classroom practice at its core (implementation and recording) but which is supported by and influences other aspects of the system.

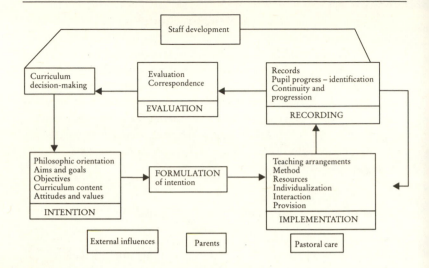

Figure 10.1 Curriculum development process

There are five categories in the area of *intention*. Philosophical orientation was often used to refer to a position that aimed towards integration. Some curriculum intentions were stated in terms of aims and goals or objectives. Curriculum content was often mentioned, as were attitudes and values that schools wished to develop in their pupils.

Formulation was intermediate between *intention* and *implementation* and was visible through the schools' curriculum documentation.

Implementation comprised six areas. Teaching arrangements (mixed ability or withdrawal) refers to the way teachers and pupils are brought together. Method refers to methods or techniques used at class, group or individual level and resources refers to curriculum materials or the lack of them. Individualization covers issues relating to individual programmes of work. The provision of staff for teaching children with learning difficulties and their interaction with other teachers were important concerns.

Recording has the following categories. Records refers to a list of records used. Pupil progress relates to the progress of children with learning difficulties and continuity and progression is the way the school ensures curriculum continuity for each child. Identification was important in mainstream schools because of the perceived need to identify children. Information from *recording* was used by teachers in classrooms, in some schools, and for this reason the *implementation* and *recording* areas are linked by an arrow intended to indicate that these two facets can operate independently of the rest of the school. On the other hand information from recording may be used in *evaluation* of the curriculum. Here evaluation (in lower case) refers to the information the school is using to make judgements about the curriculum and correspondence refers to the extent to which the curriculum received by pupils corresponds to that intended. These inform curriculum decision-making which includes the extent of teacher involvement in decisions about the curriculum.

Many teachers mentioned training courses and thus a category of staff development was created. This category also holds comments on curriculum meetings and staff discussion which were also perceived as staff development. Other aspects were also noted: pastoral care or care for the personal-social aspects of children's development; external influences, which refers to the impact of the school psychological services, the local education authority and other external agencies; and parents, which includes comments about the child's home background.

PRACTICAL IMPLICATIONS

In the school development work that followed this analysis, support was provided to teachers in representative schools to help them to develop classroom-based approaches to meet children's needs. The categories in the model were used as evaluative tools. That is, changes were looked for at these various levels. There is not space to discuss these aspects here in full, but some issues arose that were of special significance. Three of these are discussed below.

Resources, time, skills

The following factors emerged from this work as being crucial issues in the development of effective practices to meet the educational needs of children with learning difficulties. During the course of the work it became clear that resourcing the effective teaching of children with learning difficulties was a key issue. In general there was an absence of teaching materials that were relevant to the child's needs and which related to the curriculum being taught in the school. It was generally believed that it was not commercially viable for a publishing house to produce these materials and thus it was up to the teachers to do so.

Resources also need to be organized so that they can be shared, added to and developed by all teachers in the school. Space needs to be found for their storage and they need organizing and cataloguing.

The need to produce resources is one feature of the problem associated with time. In primary schools in the United Kingdom it is expected that teachers will spend all day teaching classes with relatively little time being available for other activities such as preparation. For successful integration, time is needed on the part of the teacher for discussion with other teachers (both within the school and outside it) and with parents, as well as for the preparation of materials and for planning.

Given time and a goal orientation, teachers have the main ingredients for developing their skills to meet the needs of a wider and wider range of pupils through action research methods. But both of these facets require fostering through support from the management structure and via in-service training.

Policy development

In the light of the arguments above, in order to develop the process of integration a number of directions can be taken as identified by the OECD (1995a).

- *Attitude change* Attitude change is needed on the part of teachers and school management so that children who are failing and becoming candidates for special educational provision can in principle be handled perfectly well in the mainstream school. How to deal with this issue clearly has cultural implications. It cannot be denied that attitude change is important but the means to achieve it requires extensive discussion. However, there may be little point in insisting that all children be integrated at the same time. This should be an overall goal, but the first step is to show that through modification of method and curriculum those children with relatively mild difficulties can be dealt with. The purpose of this progressive approach is to achieve success, develop practices and build on that success, always remembering that it is a whole-school approach that is required.
- *In-service training* To help to form attitudes there will be a need for in-service preparation within the context of the development of a local plan. Development of clusters of schools that can be mutually supportive is an interesting approach that has been tried successfully in the Netherlands and the United Kingdom and is one of many outlined in the OECD (1995a) report. That report also argues that in-service preparation should stress practical and

usable skills and not be too theoretical. A problem-solving approach has been found to be useful. After all, the sort of things that teachers want to and need to know is how to organize a classroom to give individual attention, how to monitor progress, how to develop materials, how to work successfully with other teachers and adults.

In-service training must not stop with teachers. It needs to be available to headteachers and others in the school. A case can be made for all school personnel to be involved, including the cleaners and caretakers. Furthermore, it should be extended to the broader group of people who manage the school including local administrators.

- *Review resources* Local administrators should review the total range of resources that are available within their school district that can be marshalled to support the schools in the development of the goal of curriculum access. This would include a careful consideration of the role of psycho-pedagogues and psychologists in this effort. These groups are a source of potential support but their efforts need co-ordinating towards developing practical skills in the school. In addition, the way in which other services need to be co-ordinated and involved in the school is also an area for development.

Pathways to progress

To address these problems a developmental package was produced, intended to help teachers and others (namely, headteachers, SEN co-ordinators, governors, advisers, educational psychologists and parents) develop a whole-school response to teaching children experiencing learning difficulties (Evans *et al.* 1989). The pack contains, among other things, practical examples as well as a video, demonstrating how teachers in primary schools can develop approaches for helping children experiencing learning difficulties make better progress largely through the development of resources, improved skills and time management.

SUMMARY AND CONCLUSIONS

In this chapter suggestions have been put forward to help in the process of conceptualizing a practical approach to developing effective educational provision, particularly for children with learning difficulties – by far the largest single group of children with SEN. First, I provided a description based essentially on a Vygotskian conception of learning which is forward-looking, action-oriented and educationally relevant. In contrast to an administrative account based primarily on medical considerations, it emphasizes school development working hand in hand with the development of teacher skills.

Second, I identified variables that are relevant to the school development enterprise and which are open to change. In brief, time is required to develop new attitudes as well as resources and skills at the level not only of the classroom but also of the school and district management.

In the third section a number of practical policy suggestions are made. These are intended to help in the establishment of practical, relevant know-how for relevant staff. The proposals recognize that what is needed is a supportive framework, emphasizing a progressive approach, which builds on success as skills are acquired. One way of implementing such an approach is through in-service resource packs for teachers and other relevant participants.

Chapter 11

Integration

A question of attitude and planning

Bjørn Glæsel

INTRODUCTION

Special education in Denmark falls into two statutory categories, each covered by the Danish 'Folkeskolelov' legislation. Section 20.1 of this deals with so-called 'normal special education'. Pupils here have milder forms of handicaps, learning disabilities or behavioural problems, while section 20.2 covers pupils with severe handicaps or disabilities. This distinction reflects the degree of special education required and the responsibility for that provision, which is in the hands of either the municipality or the county. This chapter focuses on children with severe handicaps.

A country may be judged on the basis of how it takes care of its handicapped persons. The development of care for persons with handicaps in Western Europe has been rather similar, although the organization of teaching pupils with handicaps differs markedly. The percentage of pupils being taught in special schools in the Netherlands, for example, is 4 per cent, but only 0.6 per cent in Denmark. This is not to say that the lower the percentage the better, but the difference is interesting because since the Middle Ages both countries have been influenced by similar philosophical, religious and political tendencies. The differences may nevertheless be ascribed to varying attitudes as well as to legislation and the planning of special education provision.

Denmark had been segregating pupils into special classes and schools in ways similar to most other Western countries for some 150 years, when special provision became a focus of interest and discussion. There were several reasons for this. In the 1930s and 1940s, when average class sizes were thirty-five or more, it seemed a good idea to place slow-learning pupils in special, smaller classes with a more individualized approach to pupils. As the birth rate fell, however, and the standard of living rose, class sizes dropped to less than twenty, making it possible to individualize teaching generally so that pupils with special needs could more easily remain in regular classes. Another reason was the recognition that large numbers of pupils with severe mental handicaps were invariably kept isolated in large institutions, and were not taught by teachers at all: of 5,000 of these, only half were being taught as late as 1970.

Articles, discussions and new legislation ensued, while many school-based integration projects took place. For pupils with milder forms of handicap such as slow learning (IQ 90–70) and reading retardation, a process of desegregation quietly gained momentum. Year by year the number of special classes dwindled and funding was directed towards regular schools, making it possible for them to provide clinics, support centres and special needs teachers.

Today, some 13 per cent of all school-age pupils receive special education within one year. About 11 per cent are placed in regular classes, 1 per cent in special classes in regular schools and 0.6 per cent in special schools. Approximately 1 per cent of all pupils are labelled 'severely handicapped' and most of them are taught in special schools. This means that about 0.4 per cent of pupils with severe handicaps are taught in regular classes or in special classes. As for the 1 per cent of pupils with severe handicaps, a few examples of integration projects from the 1970s may be mentioned. Six pupils with mental handicaps (IQ 70–60) were placed in one large regular school in Esbjerg and in the ensuing years a number of different learning situations were tried. The six were taught as a group for some subjects and with another class for others, while some were individually integrated into regular classes of pupils for certain periods of time. The projects were followed closely and widely debated with the result that, on the basis of these experiences, new legislation in 1980 shifted the responsibility for the teaching of pupils with severe handicaps from state level to the fourteen counties and 275 municipalities, which further enhanced the process of integration.

INTEGRATION IN DENMARK: SEVERE LEARNING DISABILITIES

Some ten years later, the Danish Ministry of Education, together with representatives from teacher, psychologist and parent organizations, initiated a review of the changed conditions for pupils with severe learning disabilities. Where and how were they taught? How did they function in school and at home?

In 1989, the first of three reports on integrating children with severe learning disabilities (approx. IQ 45–65) was published. The report (Jensen 1989) studied more than 200 individually integrated pupils (from grades 1 to 10) and focused on what integration implies in quantitative terms, the subjects pupils wholly participate in and what happens in this respect in subsequent years. Some 90 per cent of pupils fully participated in subjects such as singing, woodwork, needlework, sports and religion. In arithmetic only 57 per cent fully participated, in Danish 47 per cent and in English 34 per cent. However, the degree of participation dwindles over the years: in Danish from 60 per cent to 25 per cent and in arithmetic from about 70 per cent to 30 per cent (grades 1 to 10). Being actually present is one indication of integration. Another is whether integrated pupils follow the same curriculum as the ordinary children. Here there is the same tendency: for Danish and arithmetic it dwindles from 50 per cent to 25 per cent between grades 1 and 10. Jensen concluded that some pupils with severe learning disabilities can be taught in regular classes, while following broadly the same curriculum as their peers throughout their school careers.

In 1990, the second report (Varming and Rasmussen 1990) appeared in which teachers of forty pupils, randomly chosen from a total of 200, were interviewed in depth. On the basis of their research, the authors concluded that 'no statement in the investigation supports the notion that the ordinary school should not be the basis for the teaching of these pupils, although teachers from special schools have some reservations'. However, they also noted that few schools had developed a special education policy as such. Furthermore, few of the integrated pupils had friends among the ordinary pupils, especially in the higher grades.

The authors underlined the need for detailed individual planning for each child, including teaching goals, aims, content, methods and resources. Finding many teachers lacking sufficient knowledge, they proposed:

1 Introductory courses for teachers about to teach children with special needs.
2 Courses for all teachers at a school.
3 In-service training and supervision for specific problems arising.

TEACHING IN CLASSES WITH PUPILS WITH SPECIAL NEEDS

The study *Specialundervisningens mange ansigter* ('The many faces of special education', Frey *et al*. 1991) presents 102 developmental projects supported by the Danish Parliament in 1989/90. A number of pedagogical issues are addressed, based on in-depth interviews with teachers, pupils and parents. The main points concerning the successful teaching of small numbers of children with special needs in regular classes are:

- Special education must be an integral part of ordinary teaching.
- Group work is often preferable to individual learning. In groups of four to five, it is easier for the special needs child to be perceived as part of the group, and for the group to help this child to define and work with tasks that are relevant both to himself/herself and to the group as a whole.
- Materials produced by the teachers themselves are most important.
- All children take part in what is going on in the class as a whole.

Some of the parents of ordinary pupils are concerned whether their child receives enough relevant teaching. It is not enough that the child is kept busy doing sums or copying words. The question needs to be addressed whether regular education can be differentiated enough to encompass pupils with severe handicaps, or whether separate special education provision must also be available. The authors underline the necessity of defining clearly the roles of teachers working together in the classroom. When an extra teacher is in the classroom, it should be decided whether this extra teacher is there to support the special needs pupil or whether it is a case of teacher co-operation. They strongly advocate shared responsibility towards all pupils, planned teaching and co-operation with parents as well as other professional bodies (psychologists, social workers, and so on).

TEACHER TRAINING

While teacher training has been mentioned earlier, this needs to be given more attention. In Denmark initial teacher training, which is exclusively given in colleges and not at universities, covers wide-ranging pedagogical and psychological subjects. However, little attention is given to special needs. This means that most newly trained teachers have little or no knowledge of the needs of handicapped pupils, though students may choose it as a part of their final exam. However, there are several in-service training programmes and specific courses on offer, mainly organized by the Royal Danish School for Further Educational Studies in Copenhagen (with eight regional departments). In-service training offers teachers a choice of specializing in:

1 Specific difficulties, i.e. children with language, speech or hearing disabilities.
2 Combined difficulties, i.e. children with problems related to personality, development and social circumstances.

Training lasts for eighteen months (full-time), but is normally undertaken as a three-year part-time study. The first choice is most popular, perhaps partly because on becoming a speech therapist, teachers can more easily obtain a job, leading to easier working conditions and better pay. Denmark does have a problem here in that, while a large percentage of teachers at special schools have had additional training, this rarely includes the teaching of integrated pupils. This certainly underlines the need for in-service training as mentioned above.

THE PARENTS' VIEW

The third report, also published in 1990 (Kristoffersen 1990), presents the parents' view based on interviews. The main findings are:

- Teachers know far too little about their pupils with special needs, but they are willing to learn.
- Classmates were generally very helpful, but friendships rarely occurred.
- Social activities were a major problem for these children, and the lack of close friends with similar handicaps contributed to that.
- The greatest wish for parents was that their children achieved more self-confidence and became more socially adept.
- No clear opinion emerged on integration versus segregation. Parents generally prefer what they have chosen in the first place.

INTEGRATION

From the author's experience as a school psychologist in Frederiksborg a number of conclusions may be drawn (Glæsel 1990).

- *Blind and partially sighted pupils* With the exception of a few pupils needing medical treatment or those otherwise seriously handicapped, all these pupils are taught in regular classes. This is supported by earlier research (Ankerdal *et al.* 1986). A varying number of support lessons are required, depending on a pupil's general ability, the amount of family support and so on. Regular visits from consultants are necessary as are short courses for teachers engaging in new subjects.
- *Pupils with severe speech difficulties* The majority are taught in regular classes, although some are taught in special classes, especially in the early school years.
- *Deaf and severely hearing-impaired pupils* While a few examples of integrating pupils with hearing losses down to 70–80 db are found, it is much more common that they are taught in special schools or in classes. The main problems for integrating these pupils are related to identity-formation, especially from the age of eleven or twelve, and the need for a sign-language environment. Furthermore, integrated pupils need intensive support (the number of weekly support lessons rises from ten to eighteen lessons during their school career).
- *Severely physically handicapped pupils* Nearly all these children are integrated, although the degree of practical support varies a lot.
- *Dyslexic pupils* These children are sometimes integrated, but mostly taught in special classes. When integrated, support lessons are always necessary to varying degrees.
- *Pupils with severe learning disabilities* Added to the many findings listed above, a few points should be made: group integration seems to be by far the best model. When pupils are individually integrated, an intensive and increasing number of support lessons are necessary (from twelve to twenty per week).

CRITERIA FOR SPECIAL PROVISION

The Danish view is well put in a paper on the aims and goals for the teaching of severely handicapped children in the county of Copenhagen, seen from an administrative point of view (Hansen 1991). Both the county and representatives of its eighteen municipalities agreed that there should be a cohesive system of teaching and counselling of all children with severe handicaps. All types of provision must continue to exist, while it must be easy for a child to move from one form of teaching to another. Furthermore, the child must be taught in his/her own municipality whenever possible and referrals must be closely co-ordinated between the municipality and county.

The Ministry of Education, to which complaints on special education provision for the pupils with severe handicaps are addressed, also stresses that all types of approaches must be available: individual integrated, special classes, special schools, and so on.

FUNDING

In Denmark the costs of teaching a pupil at a special school equate with ten support lessons (depending a little on the kind of handicap). This means that advisers and parents may choose freely from the provision, without economic pressure. Local planning may, however, play a role: in some counties authorities see a decrease in the number of pupils at a given special school and may be influenced in their advice by the need to fill empty seats. The opposite may also happen from time to time. This underlines the importance of a relatively independent school assessment service, giving advice to parents solely on the perceived needs of the child.

THE PREREQUISITES OF INTEGRATION

When the possible integration of a special needs child is discussed between the parents, the school, the school psychologist and school authorities, the following important areas should be taken into account.

1 Parents should receive detailed multi-professional advice and guidance from a number of sources, including a school psychological service. Possible alternative placements should be discussed in detail. There should be agreement that the placement might be changed and is reconsidered at least once a year.
2 The school should be suited to help the child, i.e. having proper provision for the type of handicap, and – especially important – having a positive attitude towards the project.
3 The team of teachers for the given class should have accepted the task and be well informed not only of the pupil's handicap but also of the conditions of the whole process.
4 Extra resources are needed such as books, electronic equipment and means of transport.

5 Proper teacher conditions and support: each teacher is given extra time to prepare lessons (fifteen minutes per lesson); the teacher is given a small bonus in addition to a normal salary; class size may be lowered slightly; an extra support person or in some cases support teacher is needed according to a precisely defined number of weekly lessons.

6 Regular meetings with other professionals, such as consultants, school psychologists and special school teachers, are necessary, as are meetings with the teachers' council to monitor the situation in general.

7 In-service training. When needed there should be the possibility to participate in short courses at special institutions such as our newly created 'Knowledge-Centres'.

8 Careful evaluation is needed at least once a year. This could typically relate to:

- a pupil's progress in each subject viewed in the light of the planning and possible explanations of any deviation;
- a pupil's emotional development: how does the pupil see himself/herself as a member of the class and how is the pupil seen and treated by classmates?
- the changes to be made in each area: what curriculum-based goals should be set and what kinds of materials and methods are regarded as necessary?

9 Parents are very much a part of the whole process and should be informed in detail about the views of their pupils' teachers and about the school psychological service. These professionals are required by law to make every effort to explain to the parents all recommendations made for their child.

ATTITUDES – A RECENT CHANGE?

While Danish attitudes both officially and in everyday practice are quite tolerant towards persons with severe handicaps, there is a tendency towards segregation. The number of special classes is slightly increasing. This is a trend that should be monitored closely. Are today's pupils generally more demanding for our schools? Are an increasing number of ordinary children attending schools with greater demands, mirroring changing patterns of child rearing? Or do teachers refer troublesome pupils more easily?

CONCLUSIONS

In this chapter the main emphasis has been placed on attitudes and planning. The focus was mainly on children with severe handicaps: this is natural in a Danish setting, as nearly all other children have been integrated for years.

The choice of placement of a handicapped child in the school system in Denmark is first of all a question of attitude. Danish history over the last thirty years shows that the decisive factors are the wishes of the parents and the attitudes of schools and authorities. Large groups of pupils are individually integrated or integrated in small groups in regular schools. Funding is not hampering integration because the funds 'follow the child'. It is not a question of funding per se; the costs are almost the same whether a special school or integration within a regular school is chosen.

However, detailed and precise planning of the teaching, not only for one year at a time but for a long-term perspective, is of vital importance.

Chapter 12

Inclusion

Implementation and approaches

Cor J. W. Meijer, Sip Jan Pijl and Seamus Hegarty

INTRODUCTION

Inclusion is sometimes defined as the provision of appropriate, high quality education for pupils with special needs in regular schools. Whether or not this happens depends critically on teacher variables, specifically their willingness to take on this task and their ability to carry it out (Hegarty 1994). Inclusion is not just a task for teachers, however. Although much depends on the teacher's attitude towards pupils with special needs and expertise in adapting the curriculum, the inclusion of pupils with special needs requires changes at different levels in education. In the literature on inclusion numerous suggestions can be found relating to teaching and classroom practice, the organization of the school and system factors such as policy and legislation. In our introduction to this book we gave a brief overview of these suggestions.

The factors relevant to inclusion in education have been investigated and successive chapters have offered suggestions regarding the development of inclusive schools. The summaries of these chapters give overviews of the findings, but they may overwhelm by their sheer number and diversity. In this final chapter an attempt is made to integrate these findings and contribute to a conceptual framework that focuses on the various factors that have a major influence on the implementation of inclusion.

SOCIETY AND POLICY

A basis in society

The inclusion of pupils with special needs in regular education settings is not a matter just for education. Inclusion in education should be part of an encompassing development in society in which the concept of handicap and the position of people with special needs are changing (Söder, chapter 3; Stangvik, chapter 4). In this perspective they are no longer defined primarily in terms of their need of special care and treatment, which for reasons of efficiency and convenience has to be delivered in special settings, but rather are seen as citizens who have rights within society as a whole. They are entitled to ask for special services without the necessity of being segregated. Inclusion requires that everybody, regardless of disability or learning difficulty, should be treated as an integral member of society and any special services necessary should be provided within the framework of the social, educational, health and other services available to all members of society.

In education it means that pupils with special needs are entitled to have their special needs met in regular education. Inclusion stands for an educational system that encompasses a wide diversity of pupils and that differentiates education in response to this diversity. Inclusion in education can be seen as one of the many aspects of inclusion in society. It is based upon the same principles and views, and its success depends critically on the acceptance of these principles and views in society. It is not possible to create inclusive schools without a solid inclusion-oriented basis in society.

Efforts to create inclusion in education without a societal basis will result in an implementation of inclusion as a rather technical innovation. To include pupils with special needs in regular education, it is necessary to change the regular curriculum, to train teachers, to redistribute funds, to organize support services and so on. Without a basis in society it is very difficult to make these changes in education. Teachers will argue that the pupil's interests are best served elsewhere, parents will doubt the quality of the adjustments made for their child, policy-makers and administrators will be reluctant to provide the necessary support. And even if all these obstacles are surmounted, change brought about in this way will tend to have a temporary character, just for the pupils involved and only for their time at school. It may well lead to forms of 'inclusion' which entail little more than temporary, minor adjustments to the regular curriculum for particular pupils or even to organizing covert forms of segregation in regular education.

Parents

A basis in society is an important factor in making schools more inclusive, but it is not enough. Even if in society other developments towards inclusion (inclusion in work and housing) are going on and there is general support for inclusion in education, it may be necessary to contend with segregative structures within the education system: legislation, regulations for funding, the existence of separate special institutes for teacher training, special schools and, above all, long existing habits. In many cases parents, especially those of pupils with special needs, have acted as a pressure group. Their willingness to organize a lobby, to go to court, to persuade administrators and teachers and to invest in a regular school career for their children, has regularly brought about changes in education. This is amply demonstrated from experience in the Scandinavian countries, the United States and the United Kingdom (Meijer *et al.* 1994).

Policy

Societal attitudes and pressure from parents' organizations cannot be ignored by governments. If society is in favour of inclusion and parents and schools are willing to implement it in education, governments are more likely to provide the necessary policy and financial support. Sometimes it may take a great deal of time and campaigning, but if inclusion in education is to be firmly established it must be endorsed by government.

The preceding chapters have made clear how governments can act to support inclusive schools. It is important that a government, in its role as being ultimately responsible for education, clearly states that it supports inclusion (Stangvik, chapter 4; Dyson and Millward, chapter 5). It should formulate a policy statement about inclusion, making it clear to everyone involved what the goals for the educational community are. Local policy-makers, school principals and teachers then know what the government expects them to do. A clear policy statement on inclusion may act as a push in changing the attitudes of regular and special school personnel. The government can also have an important role in stimulating early developments in pilot schools. Schools that wish to implement inclusion should be supported and funded on an experimental basis. The experiences of these schools can be of use in disseminating the message that inclusion is an attainable option for other schools as well.

Funding

A major task of the government is to create the conditions for inclusion in education. In the preceding chapters (Meijer and Stevens, chapter 9) it is shown that legislation and funding can inhibit inclusion and in some cases even stimulate and reward segregation. In general, all regulations resulting in special needs provision in special schools which cannot be made available in regular schools stimulate segregation. Although legislation generally follows developments in society, it may be necessary to change legislation and funding at an early stage of development in order to prevent the existing rules from becoming a hindrance. This seems to apply to the development of inclusive schools in particular.

Another heavily debated factor is the need for additional funding to support inclusion. Some argue that inclusion in the end will result in a reduced budget for special needs as a result of having fewer expensive, segregated special schools. Others, however, claim that concentrating pupils with special needs in a special school is more efficient and cost effective. A recent OECD study (1995a) suggests that the costs of inclusive systems are lower, but that to facilitate the transition from a segregated to an inclusive system it may be prudent to make temporary additional funding available.

The region as an intermediate structure

It is essential that the implementation of an inclusion policy is delegated to local policy-makers and school principals (Porter, chapter 6). This group of actors in education operate at a level which makes it possible to influence daily practice in schools and classrooms and at the same time they are able to secure co-operation between schools, regional school support systems and special services above school level. Also, schools operate in specific regional/local circumstances that may vary across a country. It is therefore not just for central government to determine how integration should be organized or which features an integration model should have. The implementation of an inclusion policy should always be a process in which appropriate influence at the level of the community or region is guaranteed. By giving local policy-makers and school principals both the means and the authority to start a development towards inclusion in education and, in doing so, to respond to the wishes of society, a clear signal is given to teachers in both regular and special education about the need to bring about changes in education. That in itself could be a significant step in changing teachers' attitudes.

Most authors in this book have stressed the importance of this issue, drawing attention to the need to adapt to varying regional circumstances, to have clear and short lines of communication to responsible actors and to guarantee the accessibility of local key persons. Thus, without underestimating the role of the government it is clear to all the authors that the real work has to be done in daily educational practice. Fulcher (1989b) stated that: 'Government level policies do not control what happens in schools ... It is in schools that critical decisions are made which initiate integration or exclusions ... Successful integration appears to have very little to do with issuing central government policies' (18). Dyson and Millward (chapter 5) also point out that educational change is not a simple top-down process. Thus the task at the policy level is to initiate or facilitate educational change in schools. How can this be achieved? With Skrtic (1987) we feel that schools have to be approached as a sample of 'creative agents' who are continuously involved in a problem-solving process (see also Stangvik, chapter 4, and Dyson and Millward, chapter 5, with their emphasis on the school as a problem-solving team). Skrtic (1987) argues that it is this so-called 'adhocracy' approach that best facilitates educational change. In this approach small teams are given the responsibility, the means and the freedom to accomplish certain goals. The implication for education is that school teams are asked to make their school inclusive and receive access to means and (regional) facilities to do so. The adhocracy approach is contrasted with other approaches, such as the 'machine bureaucracy' approach (in which the teacher is seen as working in a production process) or the 'professional bureaucracy' approach (in which the teacher is seen as a professional working with a client group). Because these work with certain standards and fairly fixed procedures, they easily result in exclusionary solutions. Pupils with special needs do not always fit within the production process or in the well-known client group and therefore are likely to be sent to other 'machines' or 'professionals'. That results in referral to special schools or to more covert forms of segregated special education, like special classes in regular schools. In particular, the phenomenon of special classes demonstrates the wish to show movement towards inclusion to the outside world, without actually changing anything in the educational process itself.

In combining this position with the above-mentioned need to organize inclusion regionally, we feel that the adhocracy approach is best initiated and maintained by the intermediate level: the level between schools and the government. This could be the district level, the level of school clusters or any other regional level. It is the task of the workers on the intermediate level, local policy-makers and school principals, to initiate educational change by approaching schools as adhocracies.

EDUCATIONAL REFORM

Emphasis on regular education

Educational change relating to inclusion can mainly be regarded as a challenge for regular schools. Its central thrust is not towards change in special schools nor towards creating specialized approaches within regular schools. This does not mean that the consequences of inclusion in education will not be huge for special schools: teachers and other professionals working in special educational settings are being forced to change working practices and have to adapt to a new situation. However, the primary task is to achieve educational change within the regular system. How can this be done?

The curricular concept of inclusion

Schools and their teachers are the 'active agents' (Meijer and Stevens, chapter 9) who are exposed to the daily problems. They have to develop and implement plans that lead to satisfactory outcomes for themselves and for the clients of education: the pupils and their parents. All the authors in this book are quite explicit that integration is in the first place an educational reform issue. It is exactly at this point that the term integration shifts to the concept of inclusion. Mittler (1995) puts it as follows: 'In contrast with inclusion, integration or mainstreaming do not necessarily assume such a radical process of school reform' (105). To put it differently, integration is adapting the regular school curriculum to a pupil with special needs whereas inclusion is implementing a curriculum for all.

The suggestion that a clear distinction exists between pupils with special needs and other pupils is unhelpful and, in any case, invalid. Evans (chapter 10) argues that pupils' learning needs should be viewed in terms of a continuum. The concept of special educational needs itself is nothing more than an artefact of the requirement to discriminate between groups of pupils. Some need more attention, others more time, or a more individual approach and so on; the belief that all these needs are correlated and situated in certain types of pupils is naive and without foundation, as is the assumption that specialists are necessary to help most pupils with special needs. Within the traditional psycho-medical approach this view is predominant. By sharp contrast, the interactive concept of special needs implies a strong focus on the teacher and the educational process itself (Dyson and Millward, chapter 4).

The necessary adaptations in education do not apply only to a specific group of (special needs) pupils. Several authors stress the danger of approaching the inclusion concept as a placement issue. Stangvik (chapter 4) and Dyson and Millward (chapter 5) state this quite firmly. They point out that an inclusion debate in terms of resources, in the traditional educational context, may lead to the wrong solutions. In the traditional context, pupils with special needs might even be better off in segregated schools than in integrated settings.

Changes in regular schools

Most authors refer to this task as a fundamental change in the understanding of the concept of education, the role of the teachers within schools and the curriculum. Inclusion starts from the right of all pupils to follow regular education; teachers and principals should express this basic entitlement to their pupils, parents and all other participants in the network in which the schools operate. In order to realize this entitlement, education should be based on the differences between pupils; differences between pupils are at the same time the input and the output of education. As a consequence, heterogeneous grouping and multilevel instruction are the key parameters in inclusive education. The differences between pupils may never result in hierarchical streaming, nor in decisions to repeat a year or to refer a child to a full-time or long-term 'treatment' in or outside the regular school.

The curriculum framework should thus cover all pupils, but this does not imply that all pupils do the same work in the same way and at the same speed. Organization within and between classes should be flexible. Indeed, the very concept of a class is too much the result of dividing numbers of pupils by numbers of teachers (cf. Wedell

1994 for a critique). Within the comprehensive curriculum, shifts between groups should be possible and regrouping should occur frequently.

Most authors show that integration is hindered by a strongly competitive climate. Educational approaches that are largely built on comparing pupils with a certain standard or with a notional average pupil are not conducive to the integration of pupils with special needs. Heterogeneous grouping and multilevel instruction are what is required to integrate students with special needs. Glæsel (chapter 11) refers to studies which demonstrate that group integration is preferred by pupils with special needs over individual integration. A pupil with special needs sometimes feels better in classrooms where there are other pupils with special needs. This finding is consistent with the former: the more likely it is that a pupil with special needs will be judged to be an outsider, the more difficult it is to achieve inclusion.

There are other conditions necessary for achieving inclusive education. The authors in this book have underlined the main conditions at the level of the teacher, the class, the school and the district or region. We will focus on some of these here.

Teacher education is probably one of the first steps in the chain. Teachers must learn how to handle differences in the classroom. In-service arrangements are a key element of the requisite learning. Meijer and Stevens (chapter 9) argue that experiences with integration may enhance positive teacher feelings by increasing self-efficacy and professional satisfaction. This in turn benefits pupils with special needs. Tracz and Gibson (1987) demonstrate that higher personal teacher efficacy positively influences pupil achievements. Teachers who believe in themselves are more likely to see pupil behaviour as changeable, and give more feedback, and this affects pupil outcomes. Thus the experience with inclusion of students who are difficult to teach can stimulate positive teacher attitudes and abilities.

Colleagues are a rich source of motivation and learning opportunities. The support structure within schools should be based on the capacities of the team as a whole. Problem-solving is facilitated by sharing insights with colleagues and reducing teacher isolation within the school.

A cluster of schools may enhance the transfer of effective practice from one school to another. The sharing of materials, methods, knowledge and skills within a cluster is a promising option. For those pupils who need more than within-class support by the teacher, co-operation within a school cluster or a district may be advantageous.

This is particularly the case where low-incidence conditions are concerned. Such co-operation can be organized at a regional level where school support agencies and special schools work together in order to transfer knowledge and skills to the regular school and support teachers in their approach to certain pupils. Furthermore, they may provide short-term or part-time help to pupils either within the classroom or the school or, as necessary, outside the school. As pointed out, special schools and their teachers can play an important role here, but their contribution should not be built on their expert status. They are a resource for the teacher in the regular school, and all the support provided should be initiated by and organized under the responsibility of the classroom teacher or the school team.

Changes in special provision

The consequences for special schools and workers in special education have been described extensively in this book and are also elaborated in detail in reports of important projects conducted by the OECD and UNESCO (Labon, chapter 7; OECD 1995a; UNESCO 1994a). Briefly, special education has to switch from a pupil-based educational institute into a support structure or resource centre for teachers, parents and others. Its main task is to give support to regular schools, to develop materials and methods, to gather information and provide it to parents and teachers, to take care of the necessary liaison between educational and non-educational institutions, and to give support when transition from school to work takes place. In some cases special educators and special schools arrange short-term help for individual pupils or small groups of pupils. This additional support should be characterized by five simple criteria:

1 as short as possible: in order to prevent too much dependency on special arrangements and to offer opportunities to other pupils as well;
2 as soon as possible: minor problems should not have the chance to become major ones;
3 as flexible as possible: in order to modify an approach or try alternatives when a specific approach does not bring the desired results;
4 as close to home and neighbourhood school as possible: pupils

should be provided with special help without moving to other institutions or leaving their own social environment;

5 as unintrusive as possible: intervention should be as 'light' as possible, so as to minimize any negative consequences for the child.

Zigmond and Baker (chapter 8) stress that special educators have a significant role in inclusion practices and that within a full inclusion model special educators can contribute to the programme and the teaching of pupils with special needs. This may result in short-term and part-time pull-out services. They point out that fully inclusive classes do have some dangers, just as the self-contained special classes have. A continuum of services within regular education that enables individualized planning is the ideal. Sometimes forms of co-teaching are advantageous, sometimes small group or individual work is needed. There is no such thing as a single model that is effective for all pupils with special needs. This supports our argument that inclusion policy is not only a top-down issue: a great deal of flexibility is needed in order to adapt inclusion policies to local/regional circumstances and wishes.

NEW PARADIGMS IN RESEARCH ON SPECIAL NEEDS

Evaluation studies concerning the effects of inclusion show a wide range of outcomes (Söder, chapter 3). A number of studies show that inclusion is effective in terms of pupil outcomes (see OECD 1995a; special issue of the *European Journal of Special Needs Education* 8 (1993), 3). Zigmond and Baker (chapter 8) point out that separate special class placements can result in inferior outcomes. But they strongly nuance this statement by showing that short-term help in resource rooms may result in higher academic skills and at least the same self-concept outcomes. However, there are research findings that show that the effects of inclusion are not particularly promising (see, for example, Bless 1995). As is often pointed out, the methodological problems connected with this type of study (for example, the impossibility of randomly assigning pupils to treatments) make it difficult to come up with firm and clear findings. Hegarty (1993) argues that the failure of comparative studies to show a clearcut advantage in favour of segregated placements must be taken as an endorsement of integration, on the grounds that it is for segregationists to justify their case with empirical evidence.

Research within the 'effect paradigm' is based on the belief that effects are decisive with respect to the question of whether inclusion is advantageous or not and, more or less implicitly, whether inclusion should be implemented or not. Söder demonstrates quite clearly that this type of question emerges from the evaluative viewpoint. He argues that these questions do not advance us any further: not only are research findings often quite contradictory, but the level of questioning is also wrong and there are more appropriate questions to be raised. This debate is comparable with the discussion about the so-called efficacy studies in which the type of placement (mainstream versus special class or school) is the principal independent variable. Most authors now believe that this type of research is not very productive; research should focus on the nature of interventions and their specific characteristics. This is because in general people are not opposed to efforts towards integration but dispute the conditions under which it is profitable for pupils, parents and teachers. Thus, the question is not whether inclusion is possible or necessary – both are taken for granted – but under which conditions inclusion is enhanced and what kind of effects it has on pupils.

Söder and Stangvik (chapters 3 and 4) focus strongly on the long-term perspective of inclusion: the position of the handicapped in society. They feel that inclusion in education is a means for enhancing participation in society in adult life. Long-term inclusion cannot be achieved just by changing educational processes and resources. Through careful individual planning the social goals of teaching have to be taken into account within the individual perspective of the pupil with special needs. This shift in thinking has major implications for research focus and orientation. For example, the focus should be more directed to persons with special needs. Research should not try to measure effects in terms of adaptation to the environment or society without taking the situation of handicapped persons themselves into account. Research should also focus more on the type of social relations that emerge, from the perspective of the handicapped individuals themselves. This may lead to quite different conclusions about what should be achieved and how that should be done. For example, friendship relations between pupils with special needs and professionals in their environment and friendships with other pupils with special needs can be of great value (Bogdan and Taylor 1989).

Also the study of prevailing attitudes within society needs more refining. Attitudes are crucial to achieving inclusion, but research should not focus on demonstrating that attitudes are for or against inclusion but should rather give insight into the reasons for different perceptions, trace the development of these attitudes and try to analyse their effects on those with special needs and their peers. In our view, the study of attitudes has not reached that point of sophistication yet.

In conclusion, this book has shown the global compass of inclusion and the extent to which the underlying concepts are converging. Experts from many different countries are agreed in calling for a new concept of education. Inclusion should be based on the premise that children differ from each other and that these differences are fundamental to educational planning and provision.

Making schools more inclusive requires action at several levels. It is a process which depends on support from society, appropriate measures on the part of the government and the existence of support structures, in addition to reforms in the curriculum, school organization, teacher training and the provision of special services. The multi-faceted character of inclusion explains at least in part why it is difficult to implement. Making schools more inclusive will take a great deal of ingenuity, creativity and persistence on the part of all those involved. However, it is a goal worth striving for and many positive achievements have been made already. We hope that this book will help to build on these achievements and further the process of creating inclusive schools.

Bibliography

Abraham, C. (1989) 'Supporting people with a mental handicap in the community: a social psychological perspective', *Disability, Handicap and Society* 2, 4: 121–31.

Ainscow, M. (1993) 'Towards effective schools for all: a reconsideration of the special needs task', in *Seminar on Policy Options for Special Educational Needs in the 1990s* (pp. 4–18), Institute of Education, University of London.

—— (1994) *Special Needs in the Classroom: A Teacher Education Guide*, London: Jessica Kingsley Publishers/UNESCO Publishing.

Ainscow, M. and Tweddle, D. (1989) *Encouraging Classroom Success*, London: David Fulton.

Allan, J., Brown, S. and Munn, P. (1991) *Off the Record: Mainstream Provision for Pupils with Non-Recorded Learning Difficulties in Primary and Secondary Schools*, Edinburgh: Scottish Council for Research in Education.

Allen, D. (1990) 'Evaluation of a community-based day service for people with profound mental handicaps and additional special needs', *Mental Handicap Research* 2, 3: 179–95.

Ames, C. and Ames, R. (eds) (1984) *Research on Motivation in Education, Vol. 1*, San Diego: Academic Press.

Ames, C. and Ames, R. (eds) (1985) *Research on Motivation in Education, Vol. 2*, San Diego: Academic Press.

Ames, C. and Ames, R. (eds) (1989) *Research on Motivation in Education, Vol. 3*, San Diego: Academic Press.

Ankerdal, W., Johansen, M., Matthiesen-Juhl, H.C. and Påske, W. (1986) *Synshandicappede elever i almindelige klasser, specialklasser og undervisningscentre*, Undervisningsministeriets arbejdsgruppe vedr. statistik, Copenhagen.

Atkinson, D. (1988) 'Moving from hospital to the community: factors influencing the life styles of people with mental handicaps', *Mental Handicap* 16: 8–10.

Baker, J. M. (1995a) 'Inclusion in Virginia: educational experiences of students with learning disabilities in one elementary school', *The Journal of Special Education* 29: 113–23.

—— (1995b) 'Inclusion in Washington: educational experiences of students with learning disabilities in one elementary school', *The Journal of Special Education* 29: 155–62.

Ballard, K. (1995) 'Inclusion, paradigms, power and participation', in C. Clark, A. Dyson and A. Millward (eds) *Towards Inclusive Schools?* (pp. 1–14), London: David Fulton.

Barron, K. (1995) *Transition from Adolescence to Adulthood for Physically Disabled Young People*, Uppsala: Center for Disability Research, University of Uppsala.

Barton, L. and Oliver, M. (1992) 'Special needs: personal trouble or public issue?', in M. Arnot and L. Barton (eds) *Voicing Concerns: Sociological Perspectives on Contemporary Education Reforms*, Wallingford: Triangle Books.

Barton, L. and Tomlinson, S. (eds) (1984) *Special Education and Social Interests*, London: Croom Helm.

Berliner, D. C. (1989) 'Furthering our understanding of motivation and environments', in C. Ames and R. Ames (eds) *Research on Motivation in Education* (pp. 317–42), San Diego: Academic Press.

Bill 85: An Act to Amend the Schools Act (1986, June) 4th session, 50th Legislature, Province of New Brunswick, Canada.

Blalock, G. (1988) 'Transitions across the lifespan', in B. L. Ludlow, A. P. Turnbull and R. Luckasson (eds) *Transitions to Adult Status for People with Mental Retardation* (pp. 3–20), Michigan: Paul H. Brookes Publishing Company.

Bless, G. (1995) *Zur Wirksamkeit der Integration*, Berne: Verlag Paul Haupt.

Bogdan, R. and Taylor, S. (1989) 'Relationships with severely disabled people: the social construction of humanness', *Social Problems* 2, 36: 131–44.

Booth, T. (1995) 'Mapping inclusion and exclusion: concepts for all?', in C. Clark, A. Dyson and A. Millward (eds) *Towards Inclusive Schools?* (pp. 96–108), London: David Fulton.

Borkowski, J. G., Estrada, M. T., Milstead, M. and Hale, C. M. (1989) 'General problem-solving skills: relations between metacognition and strategic processing', *Learning Disabilities Quarterly* 12: 79–85.

Boyd Kjellen, G. (1991) 'The kurator system in Denmark', in OECD, *Disabled Youth: From School to Work* (pp 17–24), Paris: OECD/CERI.

Broekaert, E. and Bradt, H. (1995) *Special Education in the XXI Century, Vol. 1: Integration – School Systems*, Ghent: University of Ghent.

Brown, B. W. and Saks, D. H. (1980) 'Production technology and resource allocation within classrooms and schools: theory and measurement', in R. Dreeben and J. A. Thomas (eds) *The Analysis of Educational Productivity*, Cambridge: Ballinger.

Brown, H. and Smith, H. (1989) 'Whose "ordinary life" is it anyway?', *Disability, Handicap and Society* 2, 4: 105–19.

Bruininks, R. H. (1990) 'There is more than a zip code to changes in services', *American Journal of Mental Retardation* 1, 95: 13–15.

Calderhead, J. and Gates, P. (1993) *Conceptualizing Reflection in Teacher Development*, London: Falmer Press.

Carlberg, C. and Kavale, K. (1980) 'The efficacy of special versus regular class placement for exceptional children: a meta-analysis', *The Journal of Special Education* 14: 295–309.

Cattermole, M., Jahoda, A. and Markova, I. (1990) 'Quality of life for people with learning difficulties moving to community homes', *Disability, Handicap and Society* 2, 5: 137–53.

Centraal Bureau voor de Statistiek (1993) *Statistiek van het basisonderwijs, het speciaal onderwijs en het voortgezet speciaal onderwijs 1992/'93. Scholen en leerlingen*, 'The Hague: SDU.

Chadsey-Rush, J., Gonzales, P., Tines, J. and Johnson, J. R. (1989) 'Social ecology of the workplace: contextual variables in affecting social interactions of employees with and without mental retardation', *American Journal of Mental Retardation* 2, 94: 141–51.

Chalfont. J., Pysh, M. and Moultrie, R. (1979) 'Teacher assistant teams: a model for within-building problem solving', *Learning Disabilities Quarterly* 2, 3: 85–6.

Clark, C., Dyson, A. and Millward, A. (1990) 'Evolution or revolution: dilemmas in the post ERA management of special educational needs by local authorities', *Oxford Review of Education* 16, 3: 279–93.

Clark, C., Dyson, A., Millward, A. and Skidmore, D. (1995a) 'Dialectical analysis, special needs and schools as organizations', in C. Clark, A. Dyson and A. Millward (eds) *Towards Inclusive Schooling?* (pp. 78–95), London: David Fulton.

Clark, C., Dyson, A., Millward, A. and Skidmore, D. (1995b) *Innovatory Provision in Mainstream Schools*, London: HMSO.

Clark, C. M. and Peterson, P. L. (1986) 'Teachers' thought processes', in M. E. Wittrock (ed) *Handbook of Research on Teaching* (pp. 256–380), Chicago: Rand McNally.

Clegg, J. A. and Standen, P. J. (1991) 'Friendship among adults who have developmental disabilities', *American Journal of Mental Retardation* 6, 95: 663–71.

Collicott, J. (1991) 'Implementing multi-level instruction: strategies for classroom teachers', in G. L. Porter and D. Richler (eds) *Changing Canadian Schools: Perspectives on Disability and Inclusion* (pp. 191–218), Toronto, Ontario: The G. Allan Roeher Institute.

Commissie van de Europese Gemeenschappen (1992) *Verslag van de Commissie betreffende de voortgang van de tenuitvoerlegging van het beleid ter integratie van gehandicapten in het onderwijs in de Lid-Staten*, Brussels: Commissie van de Europese Gemeenschappen.

Corbett, J. (1994) 'Challenges in a competitive culture: a policy for inclusive education in Newham', in S. Riddell and S. Brown (eds) *Special Educational Needs Policy in the 1990s: Warnock in the Market Place* (pp. 74–91), London: Routledge.

Cordingley, P. and Kogan, M. (1993) *In Support of Education: The Functioning of Local Government*, London: Jessica Kingsley.

Cromer, R. F. (1986) 'A longitudinal study of educationally subnormal children and their acquisition of a complex linguistic structure', in J. M. Berg (ed.) *Science and Service in Mental Retardation* (pp. 197–204), London: Methuen.

Cullen, C. (1991) 'Experimentation and planning in community care', *Disability, Handicap and Society* 2, 6: 115–27.

Daniels, H. and Hogg, B. (1992) 'Report on the European exchange of experiences in school integration', *European Journal of Special Needs Education* 7, 2: 104–15.

Day, C., Pope, M. and Denicolo, P. (1990) *Insight into Teachers' Thinking and Practice*, London: Falmer Press.

Day, P. E. (1989) 'Uncertain future: experiences and expectations of people with mental handicaps of life beyond the hospital and hostel', *Mental Handicap Research* 2, 2: 166–85.

deCharms, R. (1976) *Enhancing Motivation*, New York: Irvington.

Deci, E. L. and Chandler, C. L. (1986) 'The importance of motivation for the future of the LD field', *Journal of Learning Disabilities* 19: 587–94.

Deci, E. L. and Ryan, R. M. (1985) *Intrinsic Motivation and Self-determination in Human Behavior*, New York: Plenum.

Department for Education (1994) *Code of Practice on the Identification and Assessment of Special Educational Needs*, London: Department for Education.

Deshler, D. and Schumaker, B. (1988) 'An instructional model for teaching students how to learn', in J. Graden, J. Zins and M. Curtis (eds) *Alternative Educational Delivery Systems: Enhancing Instructional Options for All Students*, Washington, DC: National Association of School Psychologists.

Donnegan, C. and Potts, M. (1988) 'People with mental handicap living alone in the community: a pilot study of their quality of life', *The British Journal of Mental Subnormality* 66, 34: 10–21.

Doornbos, K. (1969) *Opstaan tegen het zittenblijven*, The Hague: Staats-uitgeverij.

—— (1971) *Geboortemaand en schoolsucces*, Groningen: Wolters-Noord-hoff.

—— (1987) 'Een systeemkritische analyse van de groei van het speciaal onderwijs', in K. Doornbos and L. M. Stevens (eds) *De groei van het speciaal onderwijs* (pp. 94–132), The Hague: Staatsuitgeverij.

—— (1991) *Samen naar school: Aangepast onderwijs in gewone scholen*, Nijkerk: Intro.

Doornbos, K. and Stevens, L. M. (1987) *De groei van het speciaal onderwijs: Analyse van historie en onderzoek*, The Hague: Staatsuitgeverij.

Doornbos, K. and Stevens, L. M. (1988) *De groei van het speciaal onderwijs: Beeldvorming over beleid en praktijk*, The Hague: Staatsuitgeverij.

Drenth, H. E. and Meijnen, G. W. (1989) 'De positie van oud-lomleerlingen', *Tijdschrift voor Orthopedagogiek* 28: 302–20.

Dyson, A. (1990a) 'Effective learning consultancy: a future role for special needs co-ordinators?', *Support for Learning* 5, 3: 116–27.

—— (1990b) 'Special educational needs and the concept of change', *Oxford Review of Education* 16, 1: 55–66.

—— (1991) 'Rethinking roles, rethinking concepts: special needs teachers in mainstream schools', *Support for Learning* 6, 2: 51–60.

—— (1992) 'Innovatory mainstream practice: what's happening in schools' provision for special needs?', *Support for Learning* 7, 2: 51–7.

—— (1993) 'Do we need special needs co-ordinators?', in J. Visser and G. Upton (eds) *Special Education in Britain After Warnock* (pp. 98–108), London: David Fulton.

—— (1994) 'Towards a collaborative, learning model for responding to student diversity', *Support for Learning* 9, 2: 53–60.

Dyson, A. and Gains, C. (1993) 'Special needs and effective learning: towards a collaborative model for the year 2000', in A. Dyson and C. Gains (eds) *Rethinking Special Needs in Mainstream Schools: Towards the Year 2000* (pp. 155–72), London: David Fulton.

Dyson, A., Millward, A. and Skidmore, D. (1994) 'Beyond the whole school approach: an emerging model of special needs practice and provision in mainstream secondary schools', *British Educational Research Journal* 20, 3: 301–17.

Edgerton, R. B. (1967) *The Cloak of Competence: Stigma in the Lives of the Mentally Retarded*, Berkeley: University of California Press.

—— (ed.) (1984) *Lives in Process: Mildly Retarded Adults in a Large City*, Washington, DC: Monographs of the American Association on Mental Deficiency, No. 6.

Elley, W. B. (1992) *How in the World Do Pupils Read?*, Hamburg: Grindeldruck.

—— (1994) *The IEA Study of Reading Literacy: Achievement and Instruction in Thirty-two School Systems*, Oxford: Pergamon.

Elmore, R. F. (1989) 'Backward mapping: implementation research and policy decisions', in B. Moon, P. Murphy and J. Rayner (eds) *Policies for the Curriculum* (pp. 244–56), London: Hodder and Stoughton.

Emerson, E. B. (1985) 'Evaluating the impact of deinstitutionalization on the lives of mentally retarded people', *American Journal of Mental Deficiency* 3, 90: 277–88.

Espin, C., Deno, S., Maruyama, G. and Cohen, C. (1989) 'The basic academic skills samples (BASS): an instrument for the screening and identification of children at-risk for failure in regular education classrooms', paper presented at the Annual Meeting of the American Educational Research Association, San Francisco, CA.

Evans, G. and Murcott, A. (1990) 'Community care: relationships and control', *Disability, Handicap and Society* 2, 5: 123–35.

Evans, P. (1986) 'The learning process', in J. Coupe and J. Porter (eds) *The Education of Children with Severe Learning Difficulties* (pp. 183–213), Beckenham: Croom Helm.

—— (1988) 'Towards a social psychology of special education', *Educational and Child Psychology* 5: 78–90.

Evans, P., Ireson, J., Redmond, P. and Wedell, K. (1988) *Curriculum Research for Pupils with Moderate Learning Difficulties*, Final Report to the DES, London.

Evans, P., Ireson, J., Redmond, P. and Wedell, K. (1989) *Pathways to Progress*, London: Institute of Education.

Fernald, W. E. (1919) 'After-care study of patients discharged from Waverly for a period of twenty-five years', reprinted in M. Rosen, G. R. Clark and M. S. Kivitz (eds) *The History of Mental Retardation. Collected Papers, Vol. 2* (pp. 215–24), Michigan: University Park Press.

Ferrara, R. A., Brown, A. L. and Campione, J. C. (1986) 'Children's learning and transfer of inductive reasoning rules: studies of proximal development', *Child Development* 57: 1087–99.

Ferro, N. (1985) 'Integration in a secondary school, Rome', in OECD, *Integration of the Handicapped in Secondary School: Five Case Studies* (pp. 13–35), Paris: OECD/CERI.

Flynn, R. J. and Nitsch, K. E. (eds) (1980) *Normalization, Social Integration, and Community Services*, Austin, Texas: Pro-Ed, Inc.

Frey, B., Lau, J. and Skov, P. (1991) *Specialundervisningens mange ansigter*, Copenhagen: Danmarks Pædagogiske Institut.

From Being in the Community to Being Part of the Community: Summary of the Proceedings and Recommendations of a Leadership Institute on Community Integration for People with Developmental Disabilities, 21–22 November 1988, Washington, DC: The Center on Human Policy, Syracuse University.

Fuchs, D. and Fuchs, L. S. (1994) 'Inclusive schools movement and the radicalization of special education reform', *Exceptional Children* 60, 4: 294–309.

Fulcher, G. (1989a) *Disabling Policies? A Comparative Approach to Education Policy and Disability*, Lewes: Falmer Press.

—— (1989b) 'Integrate and mainstream? Comparative issues in the politics of these policies', in L. Barton (ed.) *Integration: Myth or Reality?* (pp. 6–29), London: Falmer Press.

Fullan, M. (1982) *The Meaning of Educational Change*, New York: Teachers' College Press.

—— (1991a) *The New Meaning of Educational Change* (2nd edn), London: Cassell.

—— (1991b) Preface, in G. L. Porter and D. Richler (eds) *Changing Canadian Schools: Perspectives on Disability and Inclusion* (pp. i–ii), Toronto, Ontario: The G. Allan Roeher Institute.

Gains, C. (ed.) (1994) *Collaborating to Meet Special Educational Needs*, special issue of *Support for Learning* 9, 2.

Gartner, A. and Lipsky, D. K. (1987) 'Beyond special education: toward a quality system for all students', *Harvard Educational Review* 57, 4: 367–95.

Gerber, M. M. and Semmel, M. I. (1985) 'The microeconomics of referral and reintegration: a paradigm for evaluation of special education', *Studies in Educational Evaluation* 11, 1: 13–29.

Gilkey, G. L. and Zetlin, A. G. (1987) 'Peer relations of the mentally handicapped adolescent pupils at an ordinary school', *British Journal of Mental Subnormality* 33: 50–7.

Glæsel, B. (1990) 'Vidtgående specialundervisning', I: *Håndbogen om Specialundervisning* (pp. 254–7), Gyldendal.

Good, Th. L. and Brophy, J. E. (1994) *Looking in Classrooms*, New York: Harper.

Gottlieb, J. (1981) 'Mainstreaming: fulfilling the promise?', *American Journal of Mental Deficiency* 2, 86: 115–26.

Gow, L. (1987) 'Integration or maindumping', in *Perspectives and*

Challenges: Proceedings from the 8th Asian Conference on Mental Retardation, Singapore, 14–19 November.

Gow, L., Landesman, S. and Butterfield, E. C. (1988) 'How evil are deinstitutionalization and mainstreaming? Civil rights and social science perspectives', paper presented at the Eighth World Congress of the International Association for the Scientific Study of Mental Deficiency, Dublin, August 1988.

Gustavsson, A. (1990) *Normalmiljön – det är vi det. En studie av vad det innebär att bo granne med förståndshandikappade*, Stockholm: Pedagogiska Institutionen/Centrum för kompetensutveckling i vård och omsorg.

Halliday, S. and Woolnough, L. (1989) 'Use of community facilities by adolescents with severe mental handicaps before and after moving into small staffed houses in the community', *Mental Handicap* 17: 140–4.

Halliwell, M. and Williams, T. (1993) 'Towards an interactive system of assessment', in S. Wolfendale (ed.) *Assessing Special Educational Needs*, London: Cassell.

Hansen, M. (1991) 'Den vidtgående specialundervisning i Københavns Amt', *Psykologisk Pædagogisk Rådgivning* 28: 277–300.

Hargreaves, A. (1994) 'Restructuring restructuring: postmodernity and the prospects for educational change', *Journal of Educational Policy* 9, 1: 47–65.

Hart, S. (1986) 'Evaluating support teaching', *Gnosis* (September): 26–31.

—— (1992) 'Differentiation – way forward or retreat?', *British Journal of Special Education* 19, 1: 10–12.

Hegarty, S. (1982) 'Educating pupils with special needs in the ordinary school: a comparative study of a number of integration programmes', in K. G. Stukat (ed.) *Integration: Forskning – utvecklingsarbete – praktik* (pp. 13–31), Gothenburg: Institutionen för praktisk pedagogik, Göteborgs Universitet.

—— (1991) 'Towards an agenda for research in special education', *European Journal of Special Needs Education* 6: 87–99.

—— (1993) 'Reviewing the literature on integration', *European Journal of Special Needs Education* 8, 3: 194–200.

—— (1994) 'Integration and the teacher', in C. J. W. Meijer, S. J. Pijl and S. Hegarty (eds) *New Perspectives in Special Education: A Six Country Study of Integration* (pp. 125–31), London: Routledge.

Hegarty, S., Pocklington, K. and Lucas, D. (1981) *Educating Pupils with Special Needs in the Ordinary School*, Windsor: NFER-Nelson.

Her Majesty's Inspectorate (1990) *Special Needs Issues*, London: Department of Education and Science.

Herriot, P., Green, J. M. and McConkey, R. (1977) *Organisational Memory: A Review and Project in Subnormality*, London: Methuen.

Hopkins, D. (1993) *A Teacher's Guide to Classroom Research*, Buckingham: Open University Press.

Housden, P. (1993) *Bucking the Market: LEAs and Special Needs*, Stafford: NASEN.

Hultkvist, E. (1991) 'The liaison officer in Sweden', in OECD, *Disabled Youth. From School to Work* (pp. 25–32), Paris: OECD/CERI.

Ireson, J., Evans, P., Redmond, P. and Wedell, K. (1989) 'Developing the curriculum for children with learning difficulties: towards a grounded model', *British Educational Research Journal* 15: 141–54.

Ireson, J., Evans, P., Redmond, P. and Wedell, K. (1992) 'Developing the curriculum for pupils experiencing difficulties in learning in ordinary schools: a systematic, comparative analysis', *British Educational Research Journal* 18: 155–73.

Jensen, P. E. (1989) '§19, stk. 2 elevers integration. Integrationsundersøgelsen I. Skolepsykologi', *Den Blå Serie* 12.

Johnsson, D. W. and Johnson, R. T. (1984) 'Classroom learning structure and attitudes toward handicapped students in mainstream settings: a theoretical model and research evidence', in R. L. Jones (ed.) *Attitudes and Attitude Change in Special Education: Theory and Practice* (pp. 118–42), Reston, Virginia: The Council for Exceptional Children.

Jordan, R. R. and Powell, S. D. (1994) 'Whose curriculum? Critical notes on integration and entitlement', *European Journal of Special Needs Education* 9, 1: 27–39.

Joyce, B. and Showers, B. L. (1988) *Student Achievement Through Staff Development*, New York: Longman.

Kahneman, D. (1973) *Attention and Effort*, London: Prentice Hall.

Kastner, L. S. and Repucci, N. D. (1979) 'Assessing community attitudes toward mentally retarded persons', *American Journal of Mental Deficiency* 2, 84: 137–44.

Kebbon, L., Sonnander, K., Windahl, S. I., Ericsson, K., Tideman, M. and Åkerström, B. (1992) *KOM UT-projektet. Utvärdering av kommunalisering av omsorger om utvecklingsstörda. Bakgrund och metod*, Uppsala: Centrum för handikappforskning, Uppsala Universitet.

Knuver, J. W. M. and Reezigt, G. J. (1991) *Zittenblijven in het basisonderwijs*, Groningen: RION, Instituut voor Onderwijsonderzoek.

Kobi, E. E. (1983) 'Praktizierte Integration: eine Zwischenbalanz', *Vierteljahresschrift für Heilpädagogik und ihre Nachbargebiete* 52, 2: 196–216.

Kristoffersen, G. (1990) 'Skolen og Livet. Integrationsundersøgelsen III. Skolepsykologi', *Den Blå Serie* 15.

Leijser, Y., Kapperman, G. and Keller, R. (1994) 'Teacher attitudes towards mainstreaming: a cross-cultural study in six nations', *European Journal of Special Needs Education* 9, 1: 1–15.

Leinhardt, G., Zigmond, N. and Cooley, W. W. (1981) 'Reading instruction and its effects', *American Educational Research Journal* 18: 343–61.

Lewis, J. F. (1973) 'The community and the retarded: a study in social ambivalence', in R. K. Eyman, E. C. Meyers and G. Tarjan (eds) *Sociobehavioral Studies in Mental Retardation* (pp. 164–74), Washington, DC: Monographs of the American Association on Mental Deficiency, No. 1.

Little, D. (1985) 'A crime against childhood – uniform curriculum at a uniform rate: mainstreaming re-examined and redefined', *Canadian Journal of Special Education* 2, 1: 91–107.

Lundgren, U. P. (1972) *Frame Factors and the Teaching Process: A*

Contribution to Curriculum Theory and Theory of Teaching, Gothenburg: Gothenburg Studies in Educational Sciences.

Lunt, I. and Evans, J. (1993) 'Allocating resources for special educational needs', in Seminar on Policy Options for Special Needs, Institute of Education, University of London.

Lunt, I., Evans, J., Norwich, B. and Wedell, K. (1994) *Working Together: Inter-School Collaboration for Special Needs*, London: David Fulton.

Lutfiyya, Z. M. (1991) '"A feeling of being connected": friendships between people with and without learning difficulties', *Disability, Handicap and Society* 3, 6: 233–45.

Lynch, D. (1994) *Provision for Children with Special Educational Needs in the Asia Region*, Washington, DC: The World Bank.

Maas, C. J. M. (1992) *Probleemleerlingen in het basisonderwijs*, Amsterdam: Thesis Publishers.

McConkey, R. (1990) 'Community reactions to group homes: contrasts between people living in areas with and without a group home', in W. I. Fraser (ed.) *Key Issues in Mental Retardation Research* (pp. 415–35), London: Routledge.

Madden, N. A. and Slavin, R. E. (1983) 'Mainstreaming students with mild handicaps: academic and social outcomes', *Review of Educational Research* 53: 519–69.

Mansell, J. and Beasly, F. (1990) 'Severe mental handicap and problem behaviour: evaluating transfer from institutions to community care', in W. I. Fraser (ed.) *Key Issues in Mental Retardation Research* (pp. 405–14), London: Routledge.

Marchesi, A., Echelta, G., Martin, E., Bavio, M. and Galan, M. (1991) 'Assessment of the integration project in Spain', *European Journal of Special Needs Education* 3, 6: 185–200.

Mead, G. H. (1934) *Mind, Self, and Society: From the Standpoint of a Social Behaviourist*, Chicago: University of Chicago Press.

Meijer, C. J. W. (1988) *Verwijzing Gewogen. Een studie naar de determinanten van verwijzing naar speciaal onderwijs*, Groningen: RION, Instituut voor Onderwijsonderzoek.

—— (1995) *Halverwege: van Startwet naar Streefbeeld*, De Lier: Academisch Boeken Centrum.

Meijer, C. J. W., Meijnen, G. W. and Scheerens, J. (1993) *Over wegen, schatten en sturen. Analytische beleidsevaluatie 'Weer Samen Naar School'*, De Lier: Academisch Boeken Centrum.

Meijer, C. J. W., Peschar, J. L. and Scheerens, J. (1995) *Prikkels*, De Lier: Academisch Boeken Centrum.

Meijer, C. J. W., Pijl, S. J. and Hegarty, S. (eds) (1994) *New Perspectives in Special Education*, London: Routledge.

Menolascino, F. J. and Stark, J. A. (1990) 'Research versus advocacy in the allocation of resources: problems, causes, solutions', *American Journal of Mental Retardation* 1, 95: 21–5.

Ministerie van Onderwijs en Wetenschappen (1985) *Wet op het Basisonderwijs*, The Hague: Staatsuitgeverij.

—— (1990) *Weer samen naar school. Perspectief om leerlingen ook in reguliere scholen onderwijs op maat te bieden. Hoofdlijnennotitie*, The Hague: SDU.

—— (1991) *3x Akkoord*, The Hague: SDU.

Mittler, P. (1995) 'Special needs education: an international perspective', *British Journal of Special Education* 22, 3: 105–8.

Moore, J. (1993a) 'How will the "self-managing school" manage?', in A. Dyson and C. Gains (eds) *Rethinking Special Needs in Mainstream Schools: Towards the Year 2000* (pp. 121–30), London: David Fulton.

—— (1993b) 'A response by John Moore', in P. Housden (ed.) *Bucking the Market: LEAs and Special Needs*, Stafford: NASEN.

National Center on Educational Outcomes (1993a) *Educational Outcomes and Indicators for Pupils Completing Schools*, Minnesota: NCEO, University of Minnesota.

—— (1993b) *Self-study Guide to the Development of Educational Outcomes and Indicators*, Minnesota: NCEO, University of Minnesota.

National Curriculum Council (1989a) *Circular Number 5: Implementing the National Curriculum – Participation by Pupils with Special Educational Needs*, York: National Curriculum Council.

—— (1989b) *Curriculum Guidance 2: A Curriculum for All*, York: National Curriculum Council.

Niessen, M. and Peschar, J. (eds) (1982) *International Comparative Research: Problems of Theory, Methodology and Organisation in Eastern and Western Europe*, Oxford: Pergamon Press.

Norwich, B. (1994) 'The relationship between attitudes to the integration of children with special educational needs and wider socio-political views: a US–English comparison', *European Journal of Special Needs Education* 9, 1: 91–106.

O'Connor, P. D., Stuck, G. B. and Wyne, M. D. (1983) 'Effects of a short-term interaction resource room program on task orientation and achievement', *Journal of Special Education* 13: 375–85.

OECD (1985) *Integration of the Handicapped in Secondary School: Five Case Studies*, Paris: OECD/CERI.

—— (1986) *Young People with Handicaps: The Road to Adulthood*, Paris: OECD/CERI.

—— (1988) *Disabled Youth: The Right to Adult Status*, Paris: OECD/CERI.

—— (1991) *Disabled Youth: From School to Work*, Paris: OECD/CERI.

—— (1995a) *Integrating Pupils with Special Needs into Mainstream Schools*, Paris: OECD.

—— (1995b) *Education at a Glance: OECD-indicators*, Paris: OECD.

OFSTED (1992) *Handbook for the Inspection of Schools*, London: OFSTED.

O'Hanlon, C. (1993) *Special Education in Europe*, London: David Fulton.

Oliver, M. (1990) *The Politics of Disablement*, London: Macmillan.

Orlebeke, J. F., Das-Smaal, E. A., Boomsma, D. I. and Eriksson, A. W. (1990) 'De groei van het speciaal onderwijs: een volksgezondheids-probleem', *Nederlands Tijdschrift voor Geneeskunde* 134, 27: 1315–19.

Øyen, E. (1990) 'The imperfection of comparisons', in E. Øyen (ed.) *Comparative Methodology* (pp. 1–18), London: Sage.

Padeliadu, S. and Zigmond, N. (forthcoming) 'Perspectives of students with learning disabilities about special education placement. *Learning Disabilities, Research and Practice'*.

Perner, D. (1991) 'Leading the way: the role of school administrators in integration', in G. L. Porter and D. Richler (eds) *Changing Canadian Schools: Perspectives on Disability and Inclusion* (pp. 65–78), Toronto: The G. Allen Roeher Institute.

Pijl, S. J. and Meijer, C. J. W. (1991) 'Does integration count for much? An analysis of the practice of integration in eight countries', *European Journal of Special Needs Education* 6: 100–11.

Pijl, Y. J. and Pijl, S. J. (1993) *Kenmerken van leerlingen en onderwijs in basis-, LOM- en MLK-onderwijs*, Groningen: RION Instituut voor Onderwysonderzoch.

Porter, G. L. (1986) 'School integration: Districts 28 and 29', in *Education New Brunswick* 11, 1986 (pp. 6–7), Fredericton, NB: New Brunswick Department of Education.

—— (1991) 'The methods and resource teacher: a collaborative consultant model', in G. L. Porter and D. Richler (eds) *Changing Canadian Schools: Perspectives on Disability and Inclusion* (pp. 107–54), Toronto: The G. Allen Roeher Institute.

—— (producer) (1994) *Teachers Helping Teachers: Problem Solving Teams That Work* (video), Toronto: The Roeher Institute & School District 12.

Porter, G. L. and Collicott, J. (1992) 'New Brunswick School Districts 28 and 29: mandates and strategies that promote inclusionary schooling', in R. Villa, J. Thousand, W. Stainback and S. Stainback (eds) *Restructuring for Caring and Effective Education: An Administrative Guide to Creating Heterogeneous Schools* (pp. 187–200), Baltimore, MD: Brookes Publishing Ltd.

Porter, G. L. and Richler, D. (1990) 'Changing special education practice: law, advocacy and innovation', *Canadian Journal of Community Mental Health* 9, 2: 65–78.

Porter, G. L., Wilson, M., Kelly, B. and den Otter, J. (1991) 'Problem solving teams: a thirty-minute peer-helping model', in G. L. Porter and D. Richler (eds) *Changing Canadian Schools: Perspectives on Disability and Inclusion* (pp. 219–37), Toronto: The G. Allen Roeher Institute.

Posthumus, K. (1947) *Levensgeheel en school*, The Hague: Van Hoeve.

Prillaman, D. (1981) 'Acceptance of learning disabled students in the mainstream environment', *Journal of Learning Disabilities* 14: 344–6.

Purkey, W. (1984) *Inviting School Success: A Self-concept Approach to Learning and Teaching* (2nd edn), Belmont, CA: Wadsworth Publishing Company.

Redmond, P., Evans, P., Ireson, J. and Wedell, K. (1988) 'Comparing the curriculum development process in special (MLD) schools: a systematic, qualitative approach', *European Journal of Special Needs Education* 3: 147–60.

Reezigt, G. J. and Weide, M. G. (1989) *Effecten van differentiatie, resultaten survey-onderzoek*, Groningen: RION, Instituut voor Onderwijsonderzoek.

Reynaud, G., Pfannenstiel, T. and Hudson, F. (1987) 'Park Hill secondary learning disability program: an alternative service delivery model. Implementation Manual', ERIC Document ED28931.

Reynolds, M., Wang, M. and Walberg, H. (1987) 'The necessary restructuring of special and regular education', *Exceptional Children* 53, 5: 391–8.

Richardson, S. A., Koller, H. and Katz, M. (1988) 'Job histories in open employment of a population of young adults with mental retardation', *American Journal of Mental Retardation* 29, 6: 483–91.

Roycroft, P. and Hames, A. (1990) 'Local objections to community-based houses for people with mental handicaps: factors for consideration', *Mental Handicap* 18: 11–14.

Rudduck, J. (1983) *The Humanities Project*, Norwich: School of Education, University of East Anglia Press.

Schalock, R. L., Harper, R. S. and Carver, G. (1981) 'Independent living placement: five years later', *American Journal of Mental Deficiency* 2, 86: 170–7.

School District 12 (1985) *Special Educational Services: Statement of Philosophy, Goals, and Objectives*, Woodstock, NB: School District 12.

Schulz, J. B. and Turnbull, A. P. (1984) *Mainstreaming Handicapped Students*, Newton, MA: Allyn & Bacon Inc.

Schumm, J. S. and Vaughn, S. (1991) 'Making adaptations for mainstreamed students: general classroom teachers' perspectives', *Remedial and Special Education* 12: 18–27.

Sharp, R. and Green, A. (1976) *Education and Social Control: A Study in Progressive Primary Education*, London: Routledge and Kegan Paul.

Skrtic, T. M. (1987) 'Preconditions for merger: an organizational analysis of special education reform', paper presented at the Annual Meeting of the American Educational Research Association, Washington, DC.

—— (1991a) *Behind Special Education: A Critical Analysis of Professional Culture and School Organization*, Denver, Colorado: Love Publishing.

—— (1991b) 'The special education paradox: equity as the way to excellence', *Harvard Educational Review* 61, 2: 148–206.

Slee, R. (ed.) (1993a) *Is There a Desk With My Name On It? The Politics of Integration*, London: Falmer Press.

—— (1993b) 'The politics of integration – new sites for old practices?', *Disability, Handicap and Society* 4, 8: 351–60.

—— (1995) 'Inclusive education: from policy to school implementation', in C. Clark, A. Dyson and A. Millward (eds) *Towards Inclusive Schools?* (pp. 30–41), London: David Fulton.

Söder, M. (1980) 'School integration of the mentally retarded – analysis of concepts, research and research needs', in National Swedish Board of Education (ed.) *Research and Development concerning Integration of Handicapped Pupils into the Ordinary School System* (pp. 1–30), Stockholm: National Swedish Board of Education.

—— (1987) 'Relative definition of handicap: implications for research', *Uppsala Journal of Medical Science* Suppl. 44: 24–9.

—— (1989) 'Disability as a social construct: the labelling approach revisited', *European Journal of Special Needs Education* 4: 117–29.

—— (1990) 'Prejudice or ambivalence? Attitudes toward persons with disabilities', *Disability, Handicap and Society* 3, 5: 227–41.

—— (1991) 'Theory, ideology and research: a response to Tony Booth', *European Journal for Special Needs Education* 6: 17–23.

Solum, E. and Stangvik, G. (1993) *Livskvalitet for funksjonshemmede* (Del 2. 3. opplag.), Oslo: Universitetsforlaget.

Solvang, P. (1994) *Biografi, normalitet og samfunn. En studie av handi-kappedes veier til urdanning og arbeid i Skandinavia. Avhandling for dr. polit.-graden*, Bergen: Sosiologisk Institutt, Universitetet i Bergen.

Span, B. (1988) *De kwaliteit van de onderwijskundige zorg in regulier en speciaal onderwijs*, Groningen: RION, Instituut voor Onderwijsonder-zoek.

Stainback, W. and Stainback, S. (1984) 'A rationale for the merger of special and regular education', *Exceptional Children* 51, 2: 102–11.

Stangvik, G. (1979) *Self Concept and School Segregation*, Gothenburg Studies of Educational Sciences 27, Gothenburg: Acta Universitatis Gotho-burgensis.

—— (1993) *Livskvalitet for funksjonshemmede* (Del 1. 4. opplag.), Oslo: Universitetsforlaget.

—— (1994) *Funksjonshemmede inn i lokalsamfunnet. Prinsipper of arbeidsmåter*, Oslo: Universitetsforlaget.

Stangvik, G. and Simonsen, O. (1993) *A Municipality for All Citizens: Summary and Perspectives from the Project 'Municipal competence for improvement of quality of life of handicapped persons'*, ALH: Rapport 1993: 7, Finnmark College.

Stanovich, K. E. (1986) 'Matthew effects in reading: some consequences of individual differences in the acquisition of literacy', *Reading Research Quarterly* 21, 4: 360–407.

Stenhouse, L. (1983) *Authority, Education and Emancipation*, London: Heinemann.

Stevens, L. M. (1987) 'Achtergronden van leerproblemen op relatie- en groepsniveau', in K. Doornbos and L. M. Stevens (eds) *De groei van het speciaal onderwijs: Analyse van historie en onderzoek* (pp. 74–93), The Hague: Staatsuitgeverij.

—— (1994) 'Naar een meer geïntegreerde benadering van leerstoornissen', in W. H. J. van Bon, E. C. D. M. van Lieshout and J. T. A. Bakker (eds) *Gewoon, Ongewoon, Buitengewoon* (pp. 275–97), Rotterdam: Lemniscaat.

Taylor, S. J. and Bogdan, R. (1989) 'On accepting relationships between people with mental retardation and non-disabled people: towards an understanding of acceptance', *Disability, Handicap and Society* 1, 4: 21–36.

Thompson, D. and Barton, L. (1992) 'The wider context: a free market', *British Journal of Special Education* 19, 1: 13–15.

Tomlinson, S. (1982) *A Sociology of Special Education*, London: Routledge and Kegan Paul.

Torgesen, J. K. (1977) 'The role of non-specific factors in the task performance of learning disabled children: a theoretical assessment', *Journal of Learning Disabilities* 10: 27–40.

Tøssebro, J. (1992) *Institusjonsliv i velferdsstaten. Levekår under HVPU*, Oslo: Ad Notam/Gyldendals.

Tracz, S. M. and Gibson, S. (1987) 'Teacher efficacy: its relationship to teacher time allocation, student engagement and student achievements', paper presented at the Annual Meeting of the American Educational Research Association, Washington, DC.

Turnbull, H. R. III (1991) 'The communitarian perspective: thoughts on the future for persons with developmental disabilities', unpublished paper, Beach Center on Families and Disability, University of Kansas.

UNESCO (1994a) *The Salamanca Statement and Framework for Action on Special Needs Education*, Paris: UNESCO.

—— (1994b) *World Conference on Special Needs Education: Access and Quality: Final Report*, Paris: UNESCO.

US Department of Education (1993) *Fifteenth Annual Report to Congress on the Implementation of the Individuals with Disabilities Education Act*, Washington, DC: US Department of Education.

Van den Berg, R. and Vandenberghe, R. (1988) *Onderwijsvernieuwing op een keerpunt*, Tilburg: Zwijssen.

Van Kuyk, J. J. (1990) 'Kunnen jonge kinderen "ordenen"? Onderzoek naar deelvaardigheden voorbereidend rekenen van 4–6-jarigen', *Pedagogische Studiën* 67: 429–43.

Van Rijswijk, C. M. (1986) *De hulpverlening van de LOM-school*, Amsterdam: Gemeentelijk Pedotherapeutisch Instituut.

—— (1991) 'Bestuur en beheer van geïntegreerd primair onderwijs', in K. Doornbos (ed) *Samen naar school. Aangepast onderwijs in gewone scholen* (pp. 115–35), Nijkerk: Intro.

Van Werkhoven, W., Van den Berg, C. and Stevens, L. M. (1987a) 'Afstemmingsproblemen tussen leerkracht en leerling I', *Tijdschrift voor Orthopedagogiek* 16: 21–32.

Van Werkhoven, W., Van den Berg, C. and Stevens, L. M. (1987b) 'Afstemmingsproblemen tussen leerkracht en leerling II', *Tijdschrift voor Orthopedagogiek* 16: 62–73.

Varming, O. and Elstrup Rasmussen, O. (1990) 'Integrationens børn. De gode holdninger spreder sig. Skolepsykologi', *Den Blå Serie* 14.

Vislie, L. (1995) 'Integration policies, school reforms and the organisation of schooling for handicapped pupils in western societies', in C. Clark, A. Dyson and A. Millward (eds) *Towards Inclusive Schools?* (pp. 42–53), London: David Fulton.

Vygotsky, L. S. (1978) *Mind in Society*, London: Harvard University Press.

Waerness, K. (1988) 'Comment to Mike Oliver's "Social policy and disability: the creation of dependence"', paper presented at the OECD seminar on adult status for youth with disabilities, Sigtuna, Sweden.

Walton, W. T., Rosenqvist, J. and Sandling, I. (1989) *A Comparative Study of Special Education Contrasting Denmark, Sweden and the United States of America*, Malmö: Lund University.

Ware, L. (1995) 'The aftermath of the articulate debate: the invention of inclusive education', in C. Clark, A. Dyson and A. Millward (eds) *Towards Inclusive Schools?* (pp. 127–46), London: David Fulton.

Wedell, K. (1994) 'School quality factors', paper presented at the World Conference on Special Educational Needs: Access and Quality, 7–10 June, Salamanca, Spain.

Whinnery, K. W., Fuchs, L. S. and Fuchs, D. (1991) 'General, special and remedial teachers' acceptance of behavioral and instructional strategies for mainstreaming students with mild handicaps', *Remedial and Special Education* 12: 6–17.

Wielemans, W. (1995) *Vergelijken in opvoeding en onderwijs*, Leuven/ Apeldoorn: Garant.

Will, M. (1986) 'Educating children with learning problems: a shared responsibility', *Exceptional Children* 52, 5: 411–15.

Wolfensberger, W. (1972) *Normalization: The Principle of Normalization in Human Services*, Toronto: National Institute of Mental Retardation.

—— (1985) 'Social role valorization: a new insight, and a new term, for normalization', *Australian Association for the Mentally Retarded Journal* 9, 1: 4–11.

Wood, D. J. (1980) 'Models of childhood', in A. J. Chapman and D. N. Jones (eds) *Models of Man* (pp. 227–42), Leicester: The British Psychological Society.

Zetlin, A. G. and Murtaugh, M. (1988) 'Friendship patterns of mildly learning handicapped and nonhandicapped high school students', *American Journal of Mental Retardation* 5, 92: 447–54.

Zigler, E. and Hoddap, R. M. (1986) *Understanding Mental Retardation*, Cambridge: Cambridge University Press.

Zigmond, N. (1990) 'Rethinking secondary school programs for students with learning disabilities', *Focus on Exceptional Children* 23: 1–22.

—— (1995a) 'Inclusion in Kansas: educational experiences of students with learning disabilities in one elementary school', *The Journal of Special Education* 29: 144–54.

—— (1995b) 'Inclusion in Pennsylvania: educational experiences of students with learning disabilities in one elementary school', *The Journal of Special Education* 29: 155–62.

Zigmond, N. and Baker, J. (1990) 'Mainstream experiences for learning disabled students (Project MELD): preliminary report', *Exceptional Children* 57: 176–85. ·

—— (eds) (1995) 'An exploration of the meaning and practice of special education in the context of full inclusion of students with learning disabilities', special issue of *The Journal of Special Education*, 29.

Zigmond, N., Jenkins, J., Fuchs, L., Deno, S., Fuchs, D., Baker, J. N., Jenkins, L. and Couthino, M. (1995) 'Special education in restructured schools: findings from three multi-year studies', *KAPPAN* 76: 531–40.

Index

DATE			